LOST
CIVILIZATIONS

Etruscan gold pendant. *Rapho - de Chuzgville*

440

PHILIPPE AZIZ

ETRUSCAN CIVILIZATION

"What we know today is very little compared to what we have left to learn."

Jacques de Morgan
L'Humanité préhistorique

EDITIONS FERNI

Switzerland   1979

French title:

La Civilisation étrusque

CONTENTS

I	The Mysterious Origins of the Etruscans ..	9
II	The Tragic Destiny of the Etruscans	49
III	Magi, Priests, and Diviners: Etruscan Religion	101
IV	The Resurrection of Etruria	177

THE MYSTERIOUS ORIGINS OF THE ETRUSCANS

"In this field of research, a confession of ignorance is more honorable than the pompous display of a worthless erudition."

Comte de Caylus

n December 29, 1726, the eloquent
and imposing priest Onofrio Ballelli
founded the Etruscan Academy of
Cortona, in the small Etrurian city of
Cortona.

Father Ballelli, a fine scholar of local repute, had
assembled on this solemn occasion the best minds of
Cortona and all those from near or far who displayed an
interest in their Etruscan ancestors: one hundred forty
persons in all. (1)

1. *We have freely taken our information on this Academy and its
work from Raymond Bloch,* The Ancient Civilization of the Etruscans,
*trans. James Hogarth (Geneva: Nagel, 1969). Today this work is one
of the finest reference books on the Etruscan question.*

To rescue Etruscan civilization from oblivion

"Gentlemen," declared Father Ballelli upon opening the inaugural session of the Academy, "the Romans have now been striving for more than 20 centuries to conceal or, at best, minimize the immense cultural, intellectual, political, and artistic heritage of our ancient Etruscan race! In its desire to appear as the sole civilizing influence of our peninsula, the Roman capital has always endeavored to impose an historical point of view which is far from corresponding to reality. In the seventh century B.C., when Rome was still a mere village of Latium, the Etruscan Tarquinia, Veii, Vulci, and our dear town of Cortona were already famous cities where flourished the greatest variety of arts."

Father Ballelli then painted a vast historical panorama of Etruria, praising its brilliant accomplishments in the fields of architecture, painting, and sculpture without overlooking the "wise institutions, both human and divine" which made these Etruscan cities "beacons lighting the dark night of ignorance which, in those days, reigned over the rest of Italy."

"Therefore, what is the primary purpose of our Academy?" pursued Father Ballelli. "It is both easy and difficult to achieve. Our task is to rescue our ancestors from oblivion, to make them known, to restore them to their rightful place. The resurrection of the Etruscan soul: this is our goal. Since we are clearly preparing to challenge the official history of Rome and Italy, you can be sure that we will be confronted by skepticism, mockery, and criticism of the sharpest kind.

"Each of us must be armed with patience and courage and henceforth consider himself the safe-keeper of his Etruscan heritage. We are duty bound to bring this heritage to light by searching and excavating. The countless ruins scattered throughout our region bear mute testimony to a brilliant civilization, ours. It is up to us to make the ruins speak so that they may deliver their secrets to us!"

Questions without answers

Two and a half centuries after its foundation, the Etruscan Academy of Cortona still exists, an astonishing model of continuity, perseverance, and fidelity to the spirit of its founder. With admirable consistency, it publishes memoirs, bulletins, and monographs on everything in any way related to Etruscology. The Academy's latest publication, in November 1974, presents a detailed description of the excavations in progress on Tuscan soil. (1)

Despite all these efforts, despite this remarkable tenacity, Father Onofrio Ballelli's hopes are far from fulfilled. The "resurrection of the Etruscan soul" is still at a very primitive stage!

---

1. *Note that present-day Tuscany approximately corresponds to the ancient Etruscan territory bound on the west by the Tyrrhenian Sea, on the east and south by the Tiber, and on the north by the Arno. In the course of their history, however, the Etruscans did not confine themselves to this narrow area. They extended their territory by conquests both towards the north beyond the Arno and towards the south beyond the Tiber.*

Just who were these Etruscan people? Where did they come from? When did they arrive in Italy? As for the puzzling and as yet indecipherable Etruscan language, to which linguistic group is it related? From which great race did the Etruscans spring?

These are some of the questions to which archeologists, linguists, and historians have not found satisfactory, scientifically proven answers.

Jacques Heurgon, an excellent modern specialist of Etruscology, asserts that "uncertainty, doubt, and overbold hypotheses immediately beset anyone approaching Etruscan studies." (1)

The three theories explaining the origins of the Etruscan people

The origins of the Etruscan people remain a mystery today. After two centuries of archeological excavations and linguistic, historical, and anthropological research, after the publication of hundreds of volumes and thousands of articles by French, English, German, Italian, and Russian Etruscologists in the vain attempt to resolve the baffling riddle posed by the Etruscans,

---

1. *Jacques Heurgon,* Recherches sur l'histoire, la religion et la civilisation de Capoue préromaine, des origines à la deuxième guerre punique *(Editions De Boccard, 1942). In addition to this voluminous work, Jacques Heurgon has devoted interesting monographs to Etruscan religion, divination, and several famous Etruscan individuals. We have consulted some of these to great advantage. His most recent work has been translated into English by James Kirkup as* Daily Life of the Etruscans *(New York: Macmillan, 1964).*

three theories emerge. Each has its own staunch supporters; each is based on a group of apparently sound and weighty archeological, linguistic, and historical arguments. Nevertheless, not one of them has been accepted by all Etruscologists. Among scholars and researchers, the origins of the Etruscan people are still the source of the sharpest controversies.

What then are these three basic theories?

The first holds that the Etruscans are nothing but an Indo-European people who crossed the Alps into Italy. They *initially* settled in the north of Italy, laying the foundations of the Villanovan civilization, and then descended the Apennines, ultimately settling between the Arno and the Tiber on the present-day territory of Tuscany. This is the Nordic, northern, or Indo-European thesis, which is supported by a large number of French and foreign specialists, from Jules Martha in the early 1900s to Georges Dumézil, the eminent specialist on Indo-European religions. (1)

The second theory asserts that it is useless to look beyond Italy for the origins of the Etruscan people. This is the famous so-called autochthonous (native) thesis, which is based on a text by the Greek historian, Dionysius of Halicarnassus. It also has fervent supporters, especially among Italian scholars.

Finally, the third theory maintains that the Etruscans are an Asian people whose origins hark back to Asia

---

1. *See Georges Dumézil,* Archaic Roman Religion, *trans. Philip Krapp (Chicago: University of Chicago Press, 1970). This voluminous work, the product of vast erudition, includes a large appendix on Etruscan religion.*

Minor, especially Lydia. This is the so-called oriental thesis; as the arguments that have evolved in its favor appear to be many-sided and perceptive, it now seems to be attracting the support of many Etruscologists.

Italy during the Paleolithic era

Léon Homo, one of the foremost supporters of the first thesis, reaches far back in time to find evidence for the Indo-European origin of the Etruscans.

"In Italy," he writes, "as in the rest of Europe, history, or rather prehistory, opens with the Paleolithic period; man has left the traces of his presence and activity in the diverse regions of the peninsula . . . ."(1)

Among these regions, the author mentions Liguria and Emilia. In Liguria, where archeological research has been in progress without interruption since 1850, Paleolithic dwelling places have been discovered in the caves at Balzi and Delle Fatti. The cave at Goccianello, located near the small town of Imola in Emilia, was discovered in 1869. The Po Valley, the Abruzzi, and Umbria are equally rich in archeological finds. In Umbria, for example, archeologists have discovered the remains of primitive huts, constituting an improvement over caverns, in the villages of Busco and Petrignano.

1. *Léon Homo,* Primitive Italy and the Beginnings of Roman Impe-rialism, *trans. V. Gordon Childe, 8th ed. (New York: Barnes and Noble, 1968), p. 25. Originally published in French in 1925, this work is one of the finest texts for those studying Etruscan civilization and the origins of Rome.*

Despite its primitive appearances, Paleolithic civilization is characterized by two "advanced" features: the weapon and the tool. Stylets, arrowheads and spears, as well as scissors and awls, abound in both the caverns and the huts of this period in Italy. Léon Homo notes, however, the most important shortcomings of this civilization: the absence of agriculture and stock farming.

The invention of the sewing needle

Many millennia later, the Neolithic era succeeded the Paleolithic era and polished stone replaced chipped stone. According to Léon Homo, there are also numerous vestiges of this second prehistoric era in Italy, especially in a great many caverns, such as silex toolmaking sites and implements (axes, hammers, saws, polished stones for slings, arrowheads, and spears).

Neolithic man was no longer a mere hunter or fisherman. After domesticating animals, he raised livestock and often moved from a cavern to a hut. His tools improved considerably. With the introduction of polishing techniques, deadlier and more efficient weapons were available to him (daggers, stilettos, knives, javelins). He even invented the sewing needle with an eye.

Industrial activity increased in richness and variety. Neolithic man knew how to sew clothes and work with clay. He also developed a fairly complex funerary cult. The dead were buried in a contracted position in trenches dug in open ground and containing ordinary

personal property (weapons, toilet articles, and vases).
Gradually Neolithic man acquired a social life. Men
lived clustered in villages consisting of large central
huts surrounded by smaller ones.

The Danubian heritage

According to Léon Homo, the advent of metal, in the
form of both gold and copper, marked the end of this
Neolithic era in Italy. He also mentions the countless
locations where metal first appeared during the third
millennium B.C., including the Po Valley, Lombardy,
Tuscany, and Umbria.

How was metal first introduced into Italy? By the
immigration of a highly civilized people who laid the
foundations of Etruscan culture, replies Léon Homo,
who locates the place of origin of this invading people
in the plain of the Danube, which many scholars, such
as V. Gordon Childe and Georges Dumézil, now believe
to be one of the cradles of Indo-European populations. [1]

Zacharie Mayani, a young Iranian ethnologist, has
recently revived this theory and written brilliantly in its
defense.

1. *We have gathered a great deal of information from Childe's
remarkable work,* The Dawn of European Civilization, *5th ed. (New
York: Knopf, 1951). In this volume, first published in London in 1925,
V. Gordon Childe, who held the Chair of Prehistoric European
Archeology at the University of London for many years, examines
the very slow evolution of what he calls the "Danubian civilization,"
which he considers to be one of the first manifestations of the
European genius. The group of archeological, linguistic, and religious
proofs is very impressive.*

He asserts that "the arrival of the Etruscans in Italy harks back to the third millennium B.C. when vast ethnic migrations were constantly taking place and shaping the Western world. Moreover, the oldest civilization is clearly fluvial. The true civilizers of Stone Age man were the powerful rivers of the Euphrates, the Tigris, the Nile, the Indus, and the Danube, which generously brought life to the desert, carved enormous clearings through impenetrable forests, created alluvial deposits on their banks, irrigated the lands, regulated the climate, and provided for the welfare of both man and beast."(1)

According to Mayani, the region of the Danube is the primitive place of origin of the Etruscans. Though inconclusive, the archeological evidence he presents is not devoid of interest. As a consequence of vast and complex migratory movements, black Danubian ceramic ware may be found both in Egypt and Etruria.

The great Indo-European migrations

Why and how did small Danubian tribes emigrate as far as Italy?

According to Mayani, overpopulation accounts for the emigration of these tribes (which he has identified as Illyrian or Thraco-Illyrian). Because of the exceptional fertility of their soil, the peoples of the Danube rapidly mastered agricultural techniques. The un-

1. *Zacharie Mayani,* La Fin du mystère étrusque *(Paris: Maloine, 1970).*

common prosperity these tribes enjoyed, at a time when mankind was wholly absorbed with food-gathering and hunting, was responsible for their population growth. It also allowed them to take a decisive step forward in their evolution: the discovery of bronze. When, precisely, did this discovery occur? Unfortunately, the author does not tell us.

Nevertheless, he does indicate the dates and directions of the migrations of the Danubian populations, who reached Italy only by a long detour from the east. Around the twenty-second century B.C., the Thraco-Illyrians left the Danube and headed first towards the Cyclades, the Troad, and Crete. In their wake, the Thraco-Illyrians left immense "urnfields," cemeteries where the dead were enclosed in containers and buried in graves filled with stones and earth. Six centuries later, in the sixteenth century B.C., equipped with horses and war chariots, these conquerors spread into Bosnia, Macedonia, Croatia, and Istria and reached as far as the shores of the Adriatic Sea.

According to Mayani's daring thesis, Greeks and Etruscans have the same origins. The route blazed by the victorious Thraco-Illyrians may be determined by merely consulting a map of the "urnfields" scattered in Asia Minor and the eastern Mediterranean.

Two successive Etruscan dynasties in Lydia

The Etruscans, who according to Mayani were at the time only one of many Danubian peoples, settled first in western Asia Minor, then occupied the territory of

Lydia, a rather narrow country bordered on the north by Mysia, on the east by Phrygia, on the south by Caria, and on the west by the Aegean Sea.(1)

The Etruscans, who had established roots in this area during the first centuries of the second millennium B.C., proved to be excellent builders. They founded a capital, Sardis, and several cities such as Magnesia, Tralles, and especially Tyrsa. This last city gave the Etruscans their first name. Indeed, all the historians of antiquity identify Etruscans as Tyrseni or Tyrrheni, and it was from this name as well that the sea at the western coast of the Etruscan territory in Italy became known as the Tyrrhenian Sea.

Today it is difficult to say for how many centuries the Tyrrheni or Etruscans remained in Lydia. Writers disagree on this point, as on many others. V. Gordon Childe asserts that the two partly legendary dynasties, the Atiads and the Heraclids, ruled in Lydia from the nineteenth to the thirteenth centuries B.C. On the other hand, Mayani asserts that the Heraclidan dynasty did not die out until much later, during the seventh century.

The Etruscans, Mayani writes, "settled in western Asia Minor near other Illyrian tribes. The ancients were acquainted with their city, Tyrsa. Moreover, the work of an American archeological expedition in Sardis, site of the former capital of Lydia, has helped to reveal the place names of certain Lydian settlements there,

1. *The oriental theory, based essentially on a text by Herodotus, coincides with the northern theory on this specific point. The only difference is that the northern theory considers Lydia to be a transitional stage whereas the oriental theory holds that this same region is the original home of the Etruscans.*

Grimenothura and Timenothura, for example. This discovery has led to the conclusion that *thura* means 'city' or 'fortress.' It refers to the first fortifications by which the Tyrrheni-Etruscans set themselves apart at the very dawn of their recorded history...."

According to Mayani, the Etruscans stayed in Lydia for a long time: a dozen centuries. It was six centuries according to Childe, and two or three according to another Etruscologist, Jacques Heurgon.(1) However long their stay in Lydia, the Etruscans finally joined other tribes which had settled in Asia Minor and ventured onto the open sea with them, in search of a land where they could settle permanently. In this manner they reached Egypt. The land of the Pharaohs, therefore, constitutes a midpoint between Lydia and Italy, the final port of call for the Etruscan migration before their permanent settlement in Etruria.

The Etruscans as mercenaries of the Pharaoh

The remarkable works of the Egyptologist W. Flinders Petrie are available to tell us about the presence of this mysterious people in the Nile Valley.(2)

The Etruscans of Egypt, as this eminent scholar tells us, arrived in two successive waves: the first, during the sixteenth century B.C., was peace-loving; the second, during the thirteenth century B.C., was warlike. There is nothing surprising about the initial peace-

1. The Rise of Rome to 264 B.C., *trans. James Willis (Berkeley: University of California Press, 1973).*
2. *W. Flinders Petrie,* Ilahun, Kahun and Gurob, *1889-1890.*

loving wave of immigrants, explains Petrie. Egyptian society in the second millennium B.C. was open to infiltration by foreigners, who were successfully assimilated and became artisans, farmers, or even warriors in the service of the Pharaoh.

"They were probably history's first mercenaries," speculates Petries. "These mercenaries were hired by the Pharaohs of the eighteenth dynasty (1580-1320 B.C.) and the nineteenth dynasty (1320-1200 B.C.).

"As did many other foreigners, small numbers of Etruscans came to settle in Egypt, particularly in the neighboring region of Libya, southwest of Memphis, between the Nile and the oasis of Faiyum."

The Pharaoh's head steward was Etruscan

In this region between the Nile and Faiyum, Petrie headed many excavation projects, notably in the two major villages of Kahun and Gurob, as well as in a small cemetery near the Hawara Pyramid. It was there that he unearthed some bronze artifacts dating back to the reign of Thutmose III (1505-1452 B.C.).

These artifacts, though Egyptian in form, nevertheless offer surprising details indicating an Etruscan origin. First, there is a mirror with a handle in the shape of a female nude holding a dove close to her breast, a frequent subject among the Lydian Etruscans of the same period. There are also grotesquely fashioned knives and ceramics whose motifs are more Etruscan than Egyptian. And it is in Gurob that Petrie made the most astonishing discovery of his archeologist's life: the oldest Etruscan mummy ever found.

Who is this Etruscan? None other than the head steward of the Pharaoh's palace!

This mummy was discovered in Tomb 23 at Gurob, wrapped in a decorated shroud bearing the image of the deceased. The mummy wore a large wig, with hair reaching to his waist. But this wig concealed blond hair; thus he was probably European! The inscription on the tomb identifies him as An-en-Tursha, who held the position of house-steward at the court of Ramses III around 1300 B.C. And we know from several Egyptian inscriptions that the word *Tursha* indicated the Tyrrhenians.

"We do not hesitate to link him to the Etruscan race," asserts Petrie after thorough investigation. And he adds:

"It is not really surprising that such a man could advance to such a position and be buried with all the honors and ceremonies usually reserved for Egyptians of high birth."

The Indo-Europeans attack Egypt

The steward An-en-Tursha is extraordinary testimony to the first peace-loving wave which brought Etruscans to Egypt. But, as noted above, this first wave was followed by a second warlike one. This time the Etruscans were not the only group to invade Egypt. They were part of an immense Indo-European military coalition that launched attacks against

Egypt in the thirteenth and twelfth centuries B.C.

Where did this coalition come from and exactly what peoples were included in it? Archeologists and prehistorians give divergent answers to these questions. For some, such as the German archeologist Jürgen Spanuth, this coalition consisted of a group of Indo-European peoples whom the Egyptians called the "Sea People" or the "North Sea People," meaning they came from Northern Europe. (1)

The first attacks by this formidable coalition took place during the reign of Pharaoh Seti II (1210-1205 B.C.), but the decisive confrontation occurred during the fifth year of the reign of Ramses III. Coming from Palestine and Libya, the combined forces attempted to sweep over the Egyptian borders. The frescoes at Medinet Habu depict these Indo-European invaders as barbarous warriors wearing vestlike garments, horned helmets or crowns of reeds, and armed with spears and shields. Their chieftains wore one-piece ankle-length coats fastened by two-pronged fibulae, typically northern clasps which were later adopted by the Greeks. These long-haired warriors were tall slender men with long heads, straight noses, and high foreheads, all characteristics of a northern European people.

The Indo-Europeans, including the Etruscans, were outnumbered and vanquished by Ramses III's imposing army. While some were captured others managed to escape. The Dorians reached Greece, the Pherians settled in Palestine and the Saka settled on the west

1. *J. Spanuth's theories are set forth in his book,* L'Atlantide, civilisation disparue, *especially the sixth part entitled "L'Atlantide, berceau de l'aryanisme."*

coast of Syria. As for the Etruscans, they reached Italy from the north. After crossing the Alps they settled in the Po Valley.

Raeti and Etruscans

Numerous literary and archeological documents bear witness to the Etruscan crossing of the Alps and their subsequent arrival in the Po Valley.

Among the literary documents, special note should be taken of Livy's famous passage to which proponents of the Etruscans' Indo-European origin invariably refer. In short, the Latin Historian believes that the Etruscans have the same origins as the Raeti, an Alpine tribe of northern or Aryan origin like the Pherians, the Dorians, or the Saka.

"Before the days of Roman domination," writes Livy, "Etruscan influence, both by land and sea, stretched over a wide area : how great their power was on the upper and lower seas is proved by the names of those seas, one being known by all Italian peoples as the Tuscan—the inclusive designation of the race—and the other as the Hadriatic, from the Etruscan settlement of Hatria. The Greeks know them as the Tyrrhenian and Adriatic seas.

"On each side of the Apennines they built twelve towns, the first twelve on the southern side towards the lower sea, and later the second twelve north of the range, thus possessing themselves of all the country beyond the Po as far as the Alps with the exception of the little corner where the Venetians live around the

shores of their gulf. The Alpine tribes have pretty
certainly the same origin, especially the Raetians,
though the latter have become so barbarized by their
wild surroundings that they have retained nothing of
their original character except their speech, and even
that has become debased." (1)

The dolichocephalic skulls of Bologna

The Parisian Nicolas Fréret (1688-1749), permanent
secretary of the Academy of Inscriptions and Belles-
Lettres, was the first scholar to rely on Livy's text to
uphold this theory. Fréret first observed that the
Etruscans called themselves Rasenna; he thought that
the Rasenna and the Raeti were one and the same
people.

Half a century later, the German historian Berthold-
Georg Niebuhr (1776-1831), a specialist in Indo-
European migrations, picked up and developed Fréret's
research, basing his ideas on anthropological data such
as the high frequency of given skull types found in the
tombs of the Po Basin near Bologna, particularly the
dolichocephalic, or long and narrow, skulls characteristic of the Indo-European.

Throughout the nineteenth century, numerous
scholars of various disciplines defended this northern
theory. This is notably the case of the linguists Corssen,
Lattès and Goldmann who view the Etruscan language

1. *Livy*, The Early History of Rome, *trans. Aubrey de Sélincourt
(Baltimore: Penguin Classics, 1960), Bk. V, 33 (p. 363). All quotations
from Livy's work, unless otherwise specified, are from this edition.*

as an Indo-European tongue like the other Italic languages.

"The Indo-European nature of the Etruscan language is undeniable," asserts Goldman, who believes that Etruscan—even if it is still not completely deciphered—is closely related to Latin, Umbrian, and Oscan.(1)

Necropolises and funerary practices

In his work, *Gli Etruschi e la lora civiltà* (Milan, 1932. *The Etruscans and their Civilization)*, Bartolomeo Nogara, a former professor at the University of Perugia and former executive director of the Vatican Museums, Monuments, and Galleries, based his thought both on Niebuhr's studies and on the kinds of sepulchres found, and asserted in turn that the Etruscans did indeed cross the Alps and invade Italy around the twelfth century B.C.:

"Examination of the theory that the Etruscans came from the North," Nogara writes, "will prove this theory to be more sophisticated and realistic than many others.

"Niebuhr, in his proof of this theory, began with the presence of the Raeti in the mountainous area of the central Alps. The Raeti were a tribe which Niebuhr

1. *We have gathered our information from M. Renard's remarkable article, "Nicolas Fréret et la théorie de l'origine septentrionale des Etrusques," published in the review* Latomus *(volume III, 1939). This review is issued in Brussels and published under the auspices of the Belgian Institute in Rome, the equivalent of the French School in Rome.*

believes to have issued from the Etruscans during their migratory travels across the Alps. Etruscan-related inscriptions found in the cantons of Ticino, Valtellina and Alto Adige make this quite probable. Just as the Etruscans of Capua had been the forerunners of the Etruscan confederation in its advance toward the south, so the Raeti might have formed the rear guard in the north, beyond the Apennines."

Nogara bases his theory on the excavations carried out in the nineteenth century in Emilia and Lombardy. The necropolises unearthed in these regions make it clear that the funerary rites practiced in transpadane Italy (north of the Po River) and in cispadane Italy (south of the Po) are identical to those in Etruria. While there is no need to dwell at length on Nogara's arguments, it should be noted that, in his view, the Etruscans lived in many places in the Po Valley, in Lombardy, and in Emilia, before moving south to settle in Etruria. This is proven by the fact that the funerary rites in northern Italy and those in Tuscany are identical.

The first European state in history

As noted earlier, the northern origin of the Etruscans is fervently upheld by Léon Homo, who sees in this mysterious people one branch of a vast Indo-European family that set off in search of new territory, traveling from north to south.

"We know nothing definite as to the exact route they followed," he admits, "but we can at least perceive the general features of this collective migration. Germany,

the British Isles, France, Spain, and Italy were sub-
merged thereby. Thus in Central and Western Europe a
European state was founded, and in its bosom a fusion
soon took place between the immigrants, a minority,
and the mass of the preexisting population.

"Accordingly the new state did not, strictly speaking, possess an ethnic unity any more than our modern
states . . . . This European state was apparently the first
of the great unitary organizations that our continent has
known." (1)

Villanovan civilization: recently discovered swastikas

Inside this vast "European state," the Etruscans who
had settled in the Po Valley created the first original
civilization known to have existed on Italian soil, the
Villanovan civilization (after Villanova, a village near
Bologna), more commonly known as the "Terramare
civilization." This term indicates pile-dwellings such as
those frequently discovered near the Alpine lakes.

Recent excavations in these *terramare,* carried out
in 1973 in the area around Bologna, have unearthed
funerary monuments of an Indo-European nature, as
well as battle-axes, pins with double spiral heads
originating from the Danube, double-edged razors, and
swords with broad hilts, common in the north during
this period, especially in Schleswig-Holstein. Carbon-
14 dating of some of these weapons has yielded a fairly

1. *Léon Homo,* Primitive Italy and the Beginnings of Roman Imperialism, *p. 46.*

precise date for the flowering of the Villanovan civilization, namely during the last Bronze Age, or the twelfth
century B.C.

A few years earlier, other excavations had also
revealed some vestiges of the Villanovan civilization,
which were predominantly Aryan in nature. And one of
the most frequent Aryan symbols was the swastika.

This research was undertaken in the Italian Alps by
the Eraldo Saracco speleological group of the Italian
Alpine Club, under the direction of the world-famous
archeologist Bruno Portigliatti.

"The digs were carried out at different times,"
according to the report published at the conclusion of
these expeditions. "In September 1967, in the Vallone
del Gravio, north of San Giorgio, a rectangular stone
(stele) 4.3 by 10.8 feet, completely covered with graffiti
shaped like swastikas (probably stylized anthropomorphic or zoomorphic figures), was discovered. The
cross is the most recurrent sign. The principal figures
are carved deeply and there are magico-ritual designs
next to the double-crosses.

"The remains of two buildings were discovered in
the same region after much research. They consist of a
rectangular block about 66 feet long, with an elliptical
end. It is a grandiose structure built of squared and
fitted stones, each weighing more than 220 pounds.

"In October 1968, another highly important discovery was made at an altitude of 6,740 feet. In the region
called Pian delle Cavalle a rectangular block measuring
3.3 by 13.1 feet was found. Like the one discussed
above, it was tilted slightly to the side (at an angle of
45°). Its surface was also carved with cross-shaped

symbols which could be interpreted as being stylized anthropomorphic figures. Next to them were a few small and deeply engraved discs and crescents whose meaning might be linked to the solar system."

The Italiotes, stemming from the same Indo-European roots

According to this northern theory, therefore, the Etruscans left signs of their passage through both the Po Valley and certain mountainous regions in the Alps. The Villanovan civilization is only the first manifestation of their genius on Italian soil before they came to settle permanently between the Tiber and the Arno in the territory which would bear their name.

According to this view, the Etruscans are only one of the many Italic peoples who invaded the Italian peninsula during the late Bronze Age. Those who support the northern theory maintain that the Etruscans, the Veneti, the Ligurians, the Umbrians, and the Latins are merely the various branches of a single Indo-European migration. Specialists in prehistory call all these groups "Italiotes."

"The peoples of the Terramare are in truth the Italiotes," Léon Homo writes, "and their long sojourn in the Po Valley represents the first stage of their march across the peninsula. The objects discovered in the *terramare* accordingly give us exact information about the life of the newcomers and the form of civilization that they brought with them from Central Europe—bronze, village life, the rite of cremation replacing the inhumation practiced during the preceding epoch . . . .

"The Italiotes did not enter Italy all in one block. Their immigration took the form of partial movements and successive waves. History preserves the memory of those 'sacred springs' at which the younger generations, sprouts budded-off from a common stem, set out in quest of adventures and to win fresh lands." (1)

Objections to the northern theory

Despite the numerous arguments on which this northern theory is based, Etruscologists are far from unanimous in support of it.

Accordingly, Raymond Bloch, one of the finest French representatives of current Etruscan studies, feels that the northern theory fails to explain the Etruscan phenomenon in its entirety. According to him, it involves too many implausibilities, too many gaps that neither archeology nor history is able to fill. "The point of departure of this Nordic hypothesis is the apparent connection between the name of the Raeti, the Raetians, an Alpine tribe . . . . and the name of Rasenna by which, according to the testimony of classical writers, the Etruscans described themselves. This opinion seems to find confirmation in a passage from Livy which states: 'Even the Alpine populations have the same origin as the Etruscans, particularly the Raetians. The latter have been rendered savage by the very nature of the region, so much so that they have

1. *Léon Homo, p. 49.*

preserved nothing of their ancient fatherland except the accent, and even that in a very corrupt form.'

"What actually happened here was that correct facts were used to arrive at wrong conclusions." (1)

The eminent Etruscologist explains that in fact the Etruscans did not descend from the north before establishing their home in Etruria. In fact, the opposite occurred. The Etruscans travelled north from their ancient homeland in Etruria, around the fourth century B.C. This is what Livy means when he observes: "On each side of the Apennines they built 12 towns, the first 12 on the southern side towards the lower sea, and later the second 12 north of the range, thus possessing themselves of all the country beyond the Po as far as the Alps with the exception of the little corner where the Venetians live . . ."

And to warn against the ever-present lure of the northern theory, Raymond Bloch adds: "It should be borne in mind that the northern theory constitutes the underpinning of otherwise quite substantial works which might as a result be deceptive." (The author makes this statement in reference to the works of Dumézil and Mayani.)

Asian navigators

For Raymond Bloch, therefore, the Etruscans come from Asia Minor. He views this oriental theory, based on a plethora of archeological and historical docu-

1. *Raymond Bloch,* The Etruscans *(New York: Praeger, 1960), p. 54.*

ments, as the only theory that can shed any light on the mysterious origins of the Etruscans.

"The bonds linking the Etruscans and the Far East," he writes, "seem constantly more numerous, precise, and clear." These ties are evident in the areas of art and particularly religion. A great specialist on the divining techniques of the ancient world, Raymond Bloch believes that the Etruscan seers and soothsayers were the descendants of the diviners of Asia Minor. Basing his theory on a text by the famous Greek historian Herodotus, he maintains that the ancestors of the Etruscans were Lydian navigators who arrived in Etruria around 1200 B.C.

The account given by Herodotus

Herodotus' text, mentioned by Raymond Bloch, is in fact the most valuable historical source that partisans of the Etruscan people's Asiatic origins have on which to base their theory. This text, written in the fifth century B.C., tells how the ancestors of the Etruscans left their homeland, Lydia, because of a great famine. After wandering for a long time, they came to the coasts of Italy and founded Etruria or, to be more precise, Tyrrhenia, so called in honor of the leader of the Lydians, Tyrrhenus.

"In the days of Atys," the Greek historian tells us, "there was a great scarcity throughout the land of Lydia. For some time the Lydians bore the affliction patiently, but finding that it did not pass away, they set to work to devise remedies for the evil. Various expedients were discovered by various persons; dice, huckle-bones, the ball, and all such games were invented, except checkers, the invention of which they did not claim as theirs. The plan adopted against the famine was to engage in games one day so entirely as not to feel any craving for food, and the next day to eat and abstain from games. In this way they passed 18 years. Still the affliction continued and even became more grievous. So the king determined to divide the nation in half, and to make the two portions draw lots, the one to stay, the other to leave the land. He would continue to reign over those whose lot it should be to remain behind; the emigrants should have his son Tyrrhenus for their leader. The lot was cast, and they who had to emigrate went down to Smyrna, and built themselves ships, in which, after they had put on board all needful stores, they sailed away in search of new homes and better sustenance. After sailing past many countries they came to Umbria, where they built cities for themselves and fixed their residence. Their former names of Lydians they laid aside, and called themselves after the name of the king's son, who led the colony, Tyrrhenians."(1)

Herodotus' story was later picked up by the Roman historian, Tacitus, with a few variations. In his *Annals,* Tacitus writes: "The Sardians claimed kinship with the Etruscans, quoting a decree of the latter. They explained that the original nation [Lydia], owing to its size, had been divided between the sons of King Atys— Tyrrhenus, who had been dispatched to create new

1. The Histories of Herodotus, *trans. George Rawlinson, ed. E.H. Blakeney (New York: Dutton, 1964), Bk. I, 94 (p. 50).*

homes, and Lydus, who had stayed in his fatherland—
the two countries, in Italy and Asia, taking the names of
their rulers . . . ." (1)

A close study of the chronology provided by Herodotus

Although Herodotus gives us many details on these
Tyrrheni, he does not specify the exact date of their
migration. According to some, like Raymond Bloch,
these events occured in the twelfth century B.C.; others
say the tenth century B.C.; some even place them in the
eighth century, at the beginning of the flowering of the
Etruscan civilization in Etruria.

"It has sometimes been held that Herodotus dated
the Tyrrhenian migration from Lydia to Tuscany during
the eighth century B.C.," emphasizes Jean Bérard.
"This is a mistake. Not only does Herodotus not provide
this date, he indicates a very different one. Pallottino
asserts that Herodotus dates the migration between the
Trojan War and the return to power of the Heraclids.
This date is closer to the one deduced from Herodotus'
text, but it is still too recent. Actually, separate from the
long text devoted in its entirety to the story of
Tyrrhenus, Herodotus is not satisfied with merely
confirming the fact that the Lydians' namesake was the
son of Atys and reporting that his brothers were Car and
Mysos: if he does not give us a precise date, he at least
gives us a *terminus ante quem*."

1. Tacitus on Imperial Rome, *trans. Michael Grant (Baltimore: Penguin, 1956), Bk. IV, 55 (p. 180).*

A dual Greek and oriental heritage

Unlike most supporters of the oriental theory, Jean
Bérard states that the departure of Tyrrhenus and his
companions for Etruria occurred before Asia Minor had
been colonized by the Greeks.

"Herodotus' narrative of the embarcation of Tyrrhenus and his companions at Smyrna," he writes,
"seems to imply that the Aegan coast of Asia Minor was
not yet occupied by the Greek colonies of Aeolia, Ionia,
and Doria, indicating a somewhat earlier date.

"As we will soon make clear, however, most of the
Etruscologists who support the oriental origins of the
Etruscans, basing their arguments on a large number of
epigraphical and archeological documents, hold that
the Tyrrheni left the Aegean coast of Asia Minor taking
with them a dual cultural heritage, both Greek and
Oriental."

"The miracle of Etruscan civilization," notes André
Piganiol, "is its intimate fusion of both Greek and
oriental elements. This coalescence had probably
already occurred on Asian soil." (1)

Winged animals, sphinxes and centaurs

On what archeological, epigraphical, and historical
evidence is the oriental theory based?

First, there are the Etruscan tombs. Early in the

---

1. *André Piganiol, "Les Etrusques, peuple d'Orient," in* Cahiers
d'Histoire mondiale, *vol. 1 (1953).*

8th century B.C., these tombs suddenly acquired a "striking oriental appearance," to use the expression of Jean Bérard, who cites examples such as the Campana Tomb at Veii, the *Sepolcreto della Banditaccia* in Caere, the cube-shaped tombs at Blera, the Warrior's Tomb in Tarquinia, the tombs discovered in the region of Viterbo (especially in the town of Sutri), and finally the famous tombs classified by Italian archeologists under the name *tombi degli ori* (tombs of gold), where the burial place is furnished with typically oriental sumptuousness.

"During the *tombi degli ori* period," Pericle Ducati writes, "there are no longer any stern necropolises with vases of crude clay molded by hand *(impasto)*, surrounded by archaic dishware in hammered bronze and old everyday articles for dress and ornament. Instead, the graves are very spacious, the hypogea underground burial chambers are hewn from solid rock and there are *tumuli* (earthen mounds) containing corridors, small chambers and graves (Vetulonia, Marsiliana d'Albegna) which yield a wealth of gold, silver, and ivory. The antiquated decorations consisting of simple geometric and linear arrangements gradually give way to new curvilinear decorative motifs patterned from the plant world and which delight in depicting animals living in the wilderness or whose monstrous features show a derivation from myth and fable (winged beasts, sphinxes, centaurs). A new trend of oriental fantasy is triumphant."(1)

1. *Pericle Ducati,* Le Problème étrusque *(Paris: Librairie Ernest Leroux, 1938).*

A comparison of Etruscan and Asiatic funerary monuments

In a comparative study of Etruscan funerary monuments and similar monuments in Asia Minor, a German archeologist, F. Schachermayer, has discovered a wealth of similarities and common features. He rejects the opinion that the Etruscans are the descendants of the Villanovan inhabitants of the Po Valley and instead maintains that this people actually came from the Aegean countries of Asia Minor such as Caria, Lydia, Phrygia, Armenia, and even from certain Aegean islands located near the coasts of Asia Minor, such as the island of Lemnos.

Schachermayer writes, "For the Etruscans, as well as for the inhabitants of Asia Minor, the tomb constituted the house of the deceased. This explains the richness and variety of the burial furnishings found in Etruria as well as in Lydia, Caria, or Phrygia." (1)

The German Etruscologist finds many analogies between Anatolian and Etruscan funerary monuments :

"Tumulus tombs with interior architecture : Caria, Lydia—Populonia, Vetulonia, Caere, Vulci.

"Sculptural ornament at the top of the tumulus : Caria, Lydia—Vetulonia, Vulci.

"Circular chambers, vaulted cupolas : Caria Pontus—Populonia, Vetulonia.

1. *From an article published in the* Comptes Rendus de l'Académie des Inscriptions et Belles Lettres, *1961.*

"Tombs with *dromos* (sloped, open air passage-ways): Caria, Pontus—Corneto, (1) Caere.

"Imitation stone beam: Lydia, Caria—Veii, Caere, Vulci.

"Hewn vaults with façade: Asia Minor—Etruria.

"Costly funerary gifts: Phrygia—Vetulonia.

"Bronze shield found inside: Armenia—Caere."

Further evidence linking the Etruscans with Asia Minor is to be found in their religious beliefs and practices.

The interpretation of lightning and Etruscan theology

Etruscan soothsayers also derived their interpretation of lightning from Chaldea, Assyria, and Babylon. Without dwelling on the complex but very valuable work of scholars such as Warde Fowler, G. Furlani, or S. Weinstock, let us simply say that divination from lightning and the investigatory methods followed by Etruscan soothsayers are Babylonian in origin. (2) To be sure, the division of the sky into 16 sectors, a practice peculiar to the Etruscans, cannot be found as such in the Orient. However, following Babylonian doctrine, lightning originating from the four cardinal points of

1. *Former name of the Italian town built at the site of Etruscan Tarquinia.*
2. *Those interested in the research done on divination from lightning would do well to consult the basic textbook by Albert Grenier,* Les Religions étrusques et romaines, *"Mana" collection,* Les religions de l'Europe ancienne *(Paris: Presses universitaires de France, 1948).*

the sky is observed; from this start, the sky was divided first into eight and then into 16 regions.

Furthermore, Etruscan theology is derived from the Orient. In Etruria and Chaldea the world of the gods is structurally the same.

The Etruscan god, Charun, always depicted as the most horrifying of figures, inevitably brings to mind the monstrous Chaldean devil, Labartu.

From the soothsayers of Babel to the diviners of Etruria

But it is mostly Etruscan prophecy which is deeply imbued with Chaldean divinatory practices. (1) Ample evidence has established that hepatoscopy (examination of the liver) as practiced by the Etruscans originated in Asia Minor. The famous bronze model of a liver found at Piacenza, inscribed with the names of the Etruscan gods, was probably used to train aspiring haruspices (diviners), who played an important part in Etruscan society. The Piacenza liver is in all respects comparable to the models of livers found at Mari in Mesopotomia and at Boghaz Keui among the Hittites.

1. *We have gathered our information for this short summary from the remarkable work published jointly by Fayard and Denoël in 1970,* Les Religions du Proche-Orient, *which consists of Babylonian and Hittite texts and was written by René Labet, professor at the Collège de France; André Caquot, director of the Ecole des Hautes Etudes; and Maurice Sznycer and Maurice Vieyra, of the Centre National de la Recherche Scientifique. (Part of the series entitled* Le Trésor spirituel de l'humanité, *under the general editorship of Jean Chevalier.)*

Etruscan divination, therefore, is more than just closely related to that of Babylon, and Etruscan haruspices are the direct descendants of the diviners of Babel and Assyria.

The brontoscopic calendar and the interpretation of thunder

Study of divination by the observation of thunder reveals a surprising fact. Lydus, in his treatise *De ostentis*, transcribed a brontoscopic calendar from a Greek text which he claims is based on a Latin translation of an Etruscan original by Nigidius Figulus. (1)

The brontoscopic calendar predicts the following outcomes: if there is thunder on June 13, the death of a powerful man is expected; if it occurs on June 20, civil unrest; if it thunders on May 13, the rivers will rise; thunder on December 15 means that many will go to war but few will return; if there is thunder on January 9, the king of the Orient will run great risks; if it is heard on August 19, slaves will commit crimes; thunder on September 7 means that women will have more power in the affairs of state than the weaker sex should have. The calendar provides a complete list of predictions for all the days of the year, which in this case begins on June 1 and in which every month has 30 days.

Now, according to the documents we have from Hashurbanipal's library, this is precisely the way

1. *This famous brontoscopic calendar is discussed at greater length in the chapter entitled "Magi, Priests, and Diviners."*

Babylonian calendars were constructed. The hemer-
ologies and menologies of Assyria are identical.
Moreover, an analysis of Nigidius' calendar justifies
conjecture that its origins were oriental: in the country
using the calendar, the hot season is dreaded and cool
winds welcomed, the favorable winds blow from the
east, rain is desirable although excessive rain increases
the danger of flooding, and grasshoppers are destructive. In that country, furthermore, criminals are
impaled on stakes, women intrigue with slaves, the
feared prince is a king of the Orient. To speculate that
this Etruscan text is itself the translation of a Chaldean
original does not seem rash.

When the Evil One has been destroyed

In the area of religion there are also astonishing
analogies to be drawn between Chaldean and Etruscan
theology. In the Byzantine encyclopedia called the
Suidas, we learn that anonymous Etruscan diviners
composed a world history of sorts. (1) According to
these magi, the Creator fixed the time-span of the
universe at twelve millennia. During the first millennium, he created the sky and the earth; during the
second he created the heavens; water and the seas
during the third; the sun, moon and stars during the
fourth; birds, reptiles, and four-footed creatures during

1. *For greater detail on this subject, see the excellent work mentioned
above,* Les Religions du Proche-Orient, *from which we have gathered
our information on divination. (Suidas was a Byzantine compiler
of the tenth century A.D.)*

the fifth millennium; and finally, during the sixth millennium, he created man. The Creator set aside the remaining six millennia for the existence of the human race.

This twelve-millennia system is derived from the Chaldean great year, or *dodecaeteris*, 12 of our years in length. The 12 millennia system is also referred to in a Pahlavi text of the Sassanid period, the *Bundahish*, which André Piganiol cites:

"From the beginning of creation to its end, when the Evil One will be stripped of all power, there is a span of twelve thousand years during which time will have limits. Then limited time will melt into infinity . . . ."

A final remark should be made before completing this survey of the oriental thesis. Among the various oriental groups we referred to were the Hittites. These Orientals were Indo-Europeans, even typical Indo-Europeans, as both their language and social structure clearly demonstrate. Other parallels have been drawn between the Hittites and the Etruscans: for example, the name of the sparrow hawk, an important bird in Etruscan divination, has the same root in both languages.

Perhaps the northern theory and the oriental theory are not as contradictory as it seems: the Etruscans, with their Lydian background, may very well have been Indo-Europeans just like their neighbors and contemporaries the Hittites. This would bring us back to the northern theory according to which, as noted above, the Etruscan settlement in Lydia was merely a transitional stage.

Pallottino's autochthonous (native) theory

Whatever may be said in its favor and despite its agreement with available evidence and the soundness of its arguments, the oriental theory is not universally supported. Italian Etruscologists, in particular their most prominent active scholar, Massimo Pallottino, maintain that the Etruscans were actually natives that had lived in Etruria since time immemorial. All the "oriental proofs," asserts Pallottino in his *Etruscologia*, indicate only that the Etruscans have always been linked to the peoples of Asia Minor by numerous commercial ties throughout the Mediterranean. (1)

On the strength of a text in which the Greek historian, Dionysius of Halicarnassus, (2) states that the Etruscans are natives of the Italian peninsula, Pallottino proposes a new investigatory approach to this mysterious people. Briefly summarized, his autochthonous (native) theory is as follows: it makes no sense to waste time and energy in order to prove a distant and hypothetical origin of the Etruscans when it is far more worthwhile to study the Etruscan people in the very land where they have "played out their fate."

1. *Massimo Pallottino*, Etruscologia *(Milan: Ulrico Hoepli, 1942). Available in English as* The Etruscans, *trans. J. Cremona, 2nd ed. (London, 1955; rpt. Bloomington: Indiana University Press, 1975). This second English edition, revised and enlarged, has been edited by David Ridgway and is based on the sixth Italian edition.*
2. *The passage in question states that: "It seems to me that the views of those who claim that the Etruscans did not emigrate from anywhere and have always lived in Italy are the most reasonable and accurate ... because the Etruscans are a very ancient people whose language and customs resemble those of no other group" (Roman* Antiquities, *Bk. I, 30).*

Pallottino suggests: "Now the methodological basis of our discussion must be as follows: we must consider the concept 'Etruscan' as well defined, limited, and attached to a controllable historical reality—that of a nation that flourished in Etruria between the eighth and the first centuries B.C., possessing its own language and its own customs. Various ethnic, linguistic, political, and cultural elements contributed to the formation of this historical reality, and this process must have occurred gradually, over a long period of time." (1)

Etruscan civilization: a brilliant synthesis

After indicating his method, the author of this highly important work—far too detailed to be summarized here—closely examines both the northern and oriental theories. In his view, these theories attempt to explain everything from the standpoint of the origin of the Etruscans.

Pallottino vigorously dismisses the principle of racial, psychological, and cultural interdependance. He reacts against the widespread tendency to seek a single answer to all the questions posed by Etruscan civilization and to view the problems it poses only as a function of its origins or, more precisely, as a function of a particular theory of its origins. "The facts have often been distorted in one way or another in order to support a particular opinion," he writes.

1. *Massimo Pallottino*, The Etruscans, *p. 78.*

The debate about origins, he reminds us, is of interest only when studying the beginnings of Etruscan civilization, not when studying its substance or development. To be sure, Pallottino does not deny that outside influences have enriched "Italy's oldest and most magnificent civilization." Quite the contrary, he even devotes long, captivating passages to Asiatic and Indo-European influences.

"This picture of the formation of the nation," he specifies, "is not complete without the inclusion of these elements that accompanied its first historical stages. The intellectual and artistic contacts with the east and with Greece played a preponderant role: they took place via the maritime trade routes, but probably also through direct contacts, the immigration of individuals or foreign settlements attracted by the mineral ressources of the country, the establishment of trading posts, etc." (1) Pallottino reminds us, however, that these contacts merely served to enrich an already indisputably gifted people.

To be sure, Massimo Pallottino's sound arguments do not satisfy the proponents of either the northern theory or the Asiatic theory. Sphinxlike, the origins of the Etruscans continue to elude the grasp of all theorists.

1. *Massimo Pallottino, p. 80.*

2

THE TRAGIC DESTINY OF THE ETRUSCANS

"In contrast to the history of many peoples who experienced dormant periods followed by sudden awakenings and managed to survive the vicissitudes of the evolving world, Etruscan history developed in isolation, following an outline as simple and as unyielding as that of a classical tragedy. In the first act, we have territorial expansion, military victories, economic prosperity. In the second there are two protagonists, Rome and Etruria, the first still weak and dominated by the second. In the third act, their power is in balance and a point of crisis is reached. In the fourth, a plot reversal occurs: Rome becomes dominant. Finally, the fifth act depicts the agony of the Etruscan people, its death throes and suffocation. Its place was confined to Italy, its time to the first millennium B.C. Fate had become playwright and had respected the three unities."

Alain Hus
Les Etrusques, peuple secret

2

THE TRAGIC DESTINY OF THE ETRUSCANS

n 1828, near a small village in Tuscan Maremma at the heart of ancient Etruria, a farm worker was peaceably plowing a field. The oxen were yoked to an old plow, moving forward slowly and steadily. Suddenly, in the middle of a furrow, the animals fell into a deep hole, dragging the plowman behind them.

When he managed to extricate himself, the farmer was amazed to discover that the cause of his accident was the deep excavation for an ancient tomb. Vases, pottery, and metal artifacts were heaped all around him. When he recovered from his shock and astonishment, he took a few of the newly discovered objects and carried them to his master. The owner of the lands where the plowman was working was none other than

Lucien Bonaparte, who had been made the Prince of
Canino.

The Princess of Canino wore Etruscan jewelry

The plowman's tale aroused Lucien Bonaparte's
interest. Intrigued by the unusual appearance of the
objects the man had brought to him, he called for an
excavation at the site of this freak accident.

The outcome of this research far surpassed the
Prince of Canino's wildest dreams; hundreds of richly
decorated tombs were revealed, yielding thousands of
vases, bronzes, sculptures, ambers, and a multitude of
gold jewelry. Fascinated by the beauty of some of the
jewelry and by the delicacy of the figurines, Lucien
Bonaparte attempted to trace their origins. When had
they been made? What unknown people's craftsmen
had possessed the skills to sculpt these bold-featured
faces or patiently to cut these delicately shaped jewels?
The Prince of Canino meditated at length on these
remnants of an original and masterly art, clearly distinct
from Roman or Greeek art.

Specialists of ancient art, historians, and archeologists were consulted and in turn expressed their
amazement:

"A fortunate accident has led you to the site of the
Vulci   necropolis,"   they   unanimously   declared.
"Around the seventh century B.C., Vulci was a
prosperous, powerful Etruscan city. The sculptures and
jewelry that you have shown us evoke a highly refined
art. The civilization they come from was the first great

civilization of pre-Roman Italy. Unfortunately, the Etruscan people and their civilization mysteriously disappeared early in the Christian era. Their writing remains almost indecipherable. The only sources of information we possess today are a few art objects unearthed here and there in Tuscany. Now, for the first time, we can examine and handle at our leisure a sizable collection of objects which had belonged to history's most mysterious people, the Etruscans. Prince, this discovery is of major importance for Etruscology and our knowledge of Antiquity. Please let us inform our colleagues of our findings."

News of the discovery of the Vulci necropolis spread rapidly through the capitals of Europe. Scholarly opinion was aroused. The *Bulletin de l'Institut de correspondance archéologique de Rome* was filled with articles, statements, and debates about the discoveries made in the tombs of this former Etruscan city.

A short while later, at a reception given by the Pontifical Court, the Princess of Canino made a sensational appearance adorned by sumptuous Etruscan jewelry!

Only half of Tuscany was explored during the 19th century

The amazing and unexpected discovery by the Maremma plowman triggered vast digging expeditions throughout the former territory of Etruria, which, by the first half of the nineteenth century, had deteriorated and become near wilderness.

Outside the major cities, life in Tuscany had slowed almost to a halt. A few isolated peasants tilled soil which had not been renewed for many, many centuries, and shepherds drove their meager flocks across often barren plains.

Bound by the Tyrrhenian Sea on the west, the Tiber River on the southeast and east, and the Arno River on the north, the former Etruscan territory covered less than 156 miles from north to south and 95 miles from east to west. In this narrow and, at the time, poverty-stricken area, scholars, archeologists, and sometimes even treasure-seekers lured by the hope of sudden wealth, uncovered priceless riches left by the Etruscans in their tombs!

George Dennis, the British consul and an amateur Etruscologist who traveled throughout Tuscany at this time, wrote down his impressions of this forsaken province:

"That wide region, on the frontiers of the former Tuscan and Roman States," he wrote, "is so rarely trodden by the foot of a traveler, even of an antiquary, that it can be no matter of surprise that relics of ancient art should exist there, and be utterly unknown to the world and gazed at with stupid astonishment by the peasantry, or else more stupidly unheeded. In a country almost depopulated by malaria, inhabited only by shepherds and husbandmen, and never traversed by the educated and intelligent, the most striking monuments may remain for ages unnoticed. So it was with the magnificent temples of Paestum. Though they had reared their mighty columns to the sunbeams for some three and twenty centuries, isolated in an open plain where they were visible for many a league, and standing on the seashore, where they must have served for ages as a landmark to the mariner; yet their very existence had been forgotten, till in the middle of the last century a Neapolitan painter discovered them afresh, rescuing them from an oblivion of fifteen hundred years. So in Etruria, the interesting cemeteries of Norchia and Castel D'Asso were brought to light not seventy years ago by some sportsmen of Viterbo." (1)

The indisputable traces of a bygone civilization

Speaking in particular about the discovery of the Castel D'Asso necropolis, Dennis writes:

"In a country like our own [England], it were scarcely possible that monuments of former ages, of the most striking character, should exist in the open air, be seen daily by the peasantry, and remain unknown to the rest of the world for many centuries. Yet so it is in Italy. Here is a site abounding in most imposing remains of the olden time, bearing at every step indisputable traces of a bygone civilization, scarcely six miles from the great thoroughfare of Italy, and from Viterbo, the largest city in all this district; and yet it remained unknown to the world at large till the year 1808, when Professor Orioli of Bologna, and the Padre Pio Semería of Viterbo, had their attention directed to the wonders of this glen. I am persuaded that Italy is not yet half explored . . . . In fact, ruins and remains of ancient art are of such common

1. *George Dennis,* The Cities and Cemeteries of Etruria, *2 vols., 3rd ed. (1848; rpt. London: John Murray, 1883), vol. 2, pp. 1-2.*

occurrence in Italy as to excite no particular attention . . . . The peasant knows them only as '*muraccia*,'
and he shelters his flock amid their walls, ploughs the
land around them, daily slumbers beneath their shade,
or even dwells within their precincts from year to year;
and the world at large knows no more of their existence
than if they were situated in the heart of the Great
Desert." (1)

Vast digging expeditions changed this situation and
rescued ancient Etruria from oblivion. Researchers and
archeologists from all over Europe worked relentlessly.
In the decades that followed the discoveries of the early
nineteenth century, many more Etruscan tombs were
uncovered. The most beautiful and the most luxurious
are the Regolini-Galassi Tomb at Caere, the Isis Tomb,
and the François Tomb at Vulci, the Hypogeum of the
Volumnii at Perugia, the painted tombs at Veii and
Tarquinia, and the Barberini and Bernardini tombs at
Palestrina.

The sizable number of frescoes, sculptures, and
articles of all kinds discovered in these funerary
chambers gave considerable impetus to Etruscology.

The Etruscans, the first city-builders of Italy

The Etruscans became a favorite subject of art
historians and writers. Aided by the recent archeological discoveries, historical works attempted to
penetrate their "secrets." Even literature adopted

1. *George Dennis,* Cities and Cemeteries, *vol. 1, p. 183.*

the Etruscan past as a setting for exotic, romantic tales.

In 1911, in a work entitled *L'Architecture dans l'Antiquité*, Professor F. Benoit demonstrated that the Etruscans were the first great city-builders of the Western world.

In his monumental *Histoire de l'art* written in 1949, P. Lavedan, a professor at the Sorbonne, emphasized the debt Roman architecture owes to the Etruscans, the first engineers and master-builders of antiquity.

As was the case for architecture, interest in Etruscan painting and sculpture increased as a result of the numerous Etruscan art exhibitions organized in European capitals.

On the literary side, *Sensations d'Italie* by the famous novelist Paul Bourget, a work which appeared in 1895, is a collection of travel impressions of Tuscany and Umbria. The Etruscan cities, Volterra and Chiusi, are described at length in rich and lyrical verbal flights.

For Charles Maurras, the already famous author of *Anthinéa* (1901), the Etruscan artisans "shaped the artistic style of all those who succeeded them in antiquity." Maurras further maintained that in the Renaissance "the genius of Florence was a direct outgrowth of Etruscan genius."

The Etruscans, a joyous or tragic people?

At the end of the nineteenth century, in Italy itself, the great poet Gabriele D'Annunzio described the Etruscans' tragic conception of life in his work of

1898, *La Città Morta (The Dead City)*. Their vision of the world, the writer tells us, is deeply imbued with sadness, anguish, and fatality.

The image of the Etruscans offered by the famous English novelist, D.H. Lawrence, in his book *Etruscan Places*, is entirely different. In 1930, during a trip to Etruria, Lawrence was fascinated by the beauty of the Tuscan sites and by the extraordinary vitality of the scenes depicted in Etruscan painting.

He wrote that Etruscan art expresses life itself, an exuberant and sensual life. "The natural flowering of life! It is not so easy for human beings as it sounds. Behind all the Etruscan liveliness was a religion of life, which the chief men were seriously responsible for. Behind all the dancing was a vision, and even a science of life, a conception of the universe and man's place in the universe which made men live to the depth of their capacity.

"To the Etruscan all was alive; the whole universe lived; and the business of man was himself to live amid it all. He had to draw life into himself, out of the wandering huge vitalities of the world. The cosmos was alive, like a vast creature. The whole thing breathed and stirred." (1)

The mysterious history of Etruria

The interest aroused by the Etruscan people and civilization among archeologists, historians, artists,

1. *D.H. Lawrence,* Etruscan Places *(New York: Viking Press, 1932),* pp. 82-83.

and writers, as well as the general public, has continued to the present day.

But what exactly do we know of this once-powerful people whose brilliant civilization had been concealed by the expansionary imperialism and grandeur that was Rome, a city which at its beginnings had itself endured Etruscan oppression?

The history of Etruria remains mysterious in many respects. To be sure, we now have written documents in the Etruscan language itself. But this language remains indecipherable, a major obstacle to direct historical study of the Etruscan people.

Etruscology is trying to make up for this short-coming by exploiting modern archeological data to the utmost and by conducting a critical study of ancient Greek and Latin authors who wrote the history of primitive Italy before Rome.

In attempting to establish a chronology and describe what is known about the history of the Etruscan people, we have drawn upon both contemporary research and the texts of Antiquity.

"While the Orient was displaying its wealth"

Without going back over the controversies about the origins of this people, let us simply say that the Etruscans appeared in central Italy around the end of the tenth century B.C. The newcomers initially settled on the western coast of the peninsula, then established firm roots further inland and built genuine small cities, the first in Italy.

These cities are the most remarkable innovations of the Etruscans in the Western world. They symbolize the dawn of the era of civilization in the Occident and particularly in Italy.

The Etruscan conquest thus marks a decisive step in the history of the Italian peninsula and the entire Western world. Before the arrival of this people, the contrast between the oriental basin and the occidental basin of the Mediterranean was striking, as Alain Hus has observed:

"Whereas the eastern Mediterranean offers the spectacle of the most brilliant civilizations the world has ever known, whereas Egypt, Crete, Greece, and Mesopotamia reach an astonishingly high degree of wealth and culture, the Italian peninsula remains lost in prehistoric darkness.

"While the Orient was displaying its wealth in temples and palaces at Luxor and Knossos, the Italic man was hiding in caverns. At a time when the Orient feasted on rare delicacies, was clad in luxurious fabrics, and adorned itself with sparkling jewels, Western man, covered in animal skins and empty-bellied, was hunting wild game." (1)

The gradual development of Etruria

When they landed on Italian soil, the emigrants thus had the skills, the knowledge and the material means to assert their control over a variety of semi-prehistoric

1. *Alain Hus,* Les Etrusques, peuple secret *(Meilleur Livre d'Histoire, 1960.*

tribes. But the founding and growth of the various cities which shaped Etruria was a long, involved process carried out by the Etruscans over two centuries, from the tenth to the eighth centuries B.C.

The newcomers setted first in Tarquinia, the oldest Etruscan city, located near the Tyrrhenian Sea, and then explored the coastal region and founded Veii, Caere (present-day Cerveteri), Vetulonia, and Vulci. They then proceeded inland, forcing the native peoples back toward the Apennine Mountains and founding the urban centers of Volsinii (Bolsena), Clusium (Chiusi), Perusia (Perugia), Cortona in the Tiber Basin, and Arretium (Arezzo) in the northeast near the Arno.

Gradually, over a period of nearly two centuries, city by city, region by region, the Etruscan domain—stretching from the Arno to the Tiber—was built up.

The slowness of Etruscan conquest during this initial stage can easily be explained.

At first, it seems, the Etruscans were only a small group of emigrants, a central core of leaders. Gradually, as their territory grew, they had to assimilate conquered peoples into Etruscan society. The conquerors were engaged in an actual colonization and "Etruscanization" program.

A vast program of territorial development

As they were engaged in a melting-pot operation to absorb the native population, the Etruscans implemented a vast development program in the conquered territory.

Huts and cabins disappeared, to be replaced by urban centers with brand-new houses, neatly arranged in rows. The Etruscans were remarkable engineers, skillful builders, and experienced hydraulics experts. They cleared the forests at the foot of the Apennines, drained the marshes and plains, and harnessed the rivers. Through continuous and intense work great advances were made in agriculture, trade, and industry.

Regarding industry, Etruria abounded in minerals—mainly copper and iron—which it exported to Greece, and which its own craftsmen worked in their home country, notably in Populonia on the northern coast, where the Etruscans had set up large foundries. Etruscan artisans manufactured tripods, lamps, and utensils of all kinds, which were greatly in demand in Greece and even in the Orient. Equally famous in Mediterranean countries were the jewels, ambers, and terracottas from Etruria.

Etruscan agriculture also flourished, exporting surplus products to Greece, especially cereals.

In exchange for agricultural and industrial products sent to Greece and the Orient, Etruria sought finished products, practical articles (stoppered flasks, vases), decorative items (ivories, caskets, jewels), and luxury items such as rich fabrics, perfumes, and other precious substances.

In this way, Etruria, Greece, and the Near East made up the three centers of an intense commercial trade in the Mediterranean basin.

A new, breathless, furious pace of life

The accomplishments of the Etruscans over two centuries (tenth to eighth centuries B.C.) were remarkable. Early in the seventh century B.C., Etruria's economic prosperity contrasted sharply with the poverty and primitive conditions prevailing among the Italic peoples of the surrounding regions such as Venetia, Romagna, Emilia, Umbria, and Latium.

These countries were then the boundaries of Etruria. By this time the Etruscan territory had reached its natural frontiers: the Apennines to the north and east, the Tyrrhenian Sea to the west, and the Tiber to the south.

Within this region, the integration of the Etruscan invaders with the native peoples had been completed. The Umbrian and Ligurian elements acquired the technology and way of life of an unquestionably more advanced civilization. Having been "Etruscanized," they considerably increased the human potential of Etruria. After it had become unified geographically, Etruria achieved human and ethnic unity.

Therefore, all the necessary material conditions for the birth of a great civilization were present. Indeed, at the opening of the seventh century B.C., Etruscan civilization suddenly flourished.

This sudden emergence, of an astonishing magnitude, is described by Sibylle von Cles-Reden in the following terms: "The slow evolution of centuries abruptly gives place to a dynamic force which sweeps them along at an almost dizzy speed. The Etruscans seem to have set out to absorb in a few decades what

other peoples had taken thousands of years to
acquire . . . . A new cult of the dead was adopted by the
inhabitants of the Tyrrhenian coast, and from that date
onward a series of magnificent tombs begins to appear
as landmarks of their lightning advance towards
civilization. From the maritime cities of the Etruscans
sprang a civilization which fused Tuscany, Latium, and
Umbria in the crucible of a common religious and
cultural system. The confederation of these cities can
be regarded as a precursor, many centuries in advance,
of that unification which Rome later imposed on the
peninsula." (1)

They ruled over land and sea

As Sibylle von Cles-Reden quite rightly emphasizes,
the economic development of Tuscany and the growth
of its population called for a coherent domestic political
structure. Unfortunately, we have very sparse information about the political organization of Etruria at this
time.

At most we know that each city-state was put under
the authority of a prince, or *lucumon*. The country itself
consisted of 12 city-states including Arretium, Caere,
Cortona, Tarquinia, Vulci, Volterra (south of the lower
Arno), and Volsinii.

1. *Sibylle von Cles-Reden,* The Buried People, a Study of the Etruscan
World, *trans. C.M. Woodhouse (London: Rupert Hart-Davis, 1955),
p. 22. Originally published in Germany as* Das versunkene Volk, *this
book sheds a typically Germanic light on Etruscan civilization,
presenting the Etruscans in a clearly Wagnerian atmosphere, bathed
in the mists and mystery dear to German romanticism.*

Bronze statuette of the God Mars as a fighting warrior (fifth century B.C.).
Archeological Museum of Florence. *(Giraudon-Lauros)*

Terracotta head, life size, of the God Hermes. One of the acroteria from the *col*
of the temple of Apollo at Veii. About 500 B.C. Villa Giulia Museum,
(Giraudon)

Built on solid economic grounds and buttressed by a political apparatus sufficiently powerful to maintain both unity and freedom of action, Etruria emerged as a dominant force in Italy. Classical authors have preserved the memory of this mastery. Cato tells us that the Etruscans once held sway over nearly all of the Italian peninsula. Livy, for once, forgot the nationalistic pride typical of a Roman historian and praised Etruria as the first major power ever to emerge in Italy.

"Before the days of Roman domination," he wrote, "Etruscan influence, both by land and sea, stretched over a wide area: how great their power was on the upper and lower seas in proved by the names of those seas which make Italy a peninsula...."

The Greco-Etruscan confrontation

As a powerful and prosperous nation on the Italian peninsula, Etruria increased its commercial and political exchanges with the great centers of the Mediterranean—Greece, Phenicia, Carthage. And it is thanks to the Etruscans that Italy was opened to outside influences.

"Etruria was in touch with the great centers of Mediterranean civilization," the historian Léon Homo writes, "and began to assume her function as leader of progress in central Italy—a function she was destined to retain and which constituted her true originality." (1)

1. *Homo,* Primitive Italy and the Beginnings of Roman Imperialism, *p. 62.*

The only rivals of the Etruscans on the peninsula were the Greeks, established since the eighth century on the southern coast as well as in Sicily. Many Greek colonies were founded there : Cumae, the first colony of Magna Graecia, (1) was followed by Naxos, Syracuse, Catania, Megara, Metapontum, Pandosia, Sybaris, Crotona, Tarentum, etc.

The Greek emigrants were representatives of a highly evolved civilization that had prospered on the shores of the Aegean Sea for many centuries. To Italy they brought their way of life, their philosophy, their city-dwelling, their technology and, above all, the alphabet, an invention hitherto unknown in Italy.

The Greek colonies rapidly grew prosperous and acquired great political stature as well. Nevertheless, Greek influence did not deeply penetrate the Italic territory and peoples. The Greeks confined their activity to establishing themselves firmly on the coast, driving the native population inland.

The situation in Italy at the end of the eighth century and at the beginning of the seventh century B.C. amounted to a confrontation between the Greeks and Etruscans. From the midst of many backward tribes there had emerged two great centers of civilization, Etruria in central Italy and Magna Graecia in the south and Sicily. Their interests inevitably came into conflict.

1. *This was the name given to the group of Greek colonies in southern Italy and Sicily.*

Etruscan expansion

The war between Etruscans and Greeks took place early in the seventh century B.C. The Etruscans, expanding at a steady pace, set out to conquer new lands and find new commercial outlets. The prosperous Greek markets were their first targets.

From the seventh to the fifth centuries B.C., the Etruscans were advancing in three directions: south towards southern Italy (i.e., Magna Graecia), west towards the occidental basin of the Mediterranean, and north in the direction of the Po Valley.

However, this Etruscan expansion was by no means the joint action of all the Etruscan *lucumonies* (city-states); it was the result of separate groups of city-states working on their own behalf. The southward expansion was led by the southern metropolises of Tarquinia, Caere, Vulci, and Veii, whereas the northward expansion was led by Volterra, Arretium, and even Cortona.

The first Etruscan thrust began in Tarquinia and Caere; there Tuscans were challenged first by the tribes of Latium, (1) then by the Greeks of Campania. Campania, the hinterland of the Greek colonies at Cumae and Naples, was justifiably famous for its agricultural wealth and its livestock. After attempting to seize the Greek cities, where the Etruscans had come face to face with a more powerful adversary, they retreated to the hinterland of Campania. For more than

1. *The Etruscan conquest of Latium is an important episode in their history, for it is closely related to the little known history of the origins of Rome. We will deal with this subject later.*

a century, the Etruscans occupied Campania, spo-
radically but unsuccessfully attacking the coastal cities.
At the end of the sixth century, a major defeat of the
Etruscan army at the hands of the Greek colony of
Cumae effectively blocked further Etruscan expansion
in southern Italy.

Breaking free at any cost

Though they were unsuccessful in establishing a
powerful foothold on the coasts of southern Italy during
this period, the Etruscans were nevertheless able to
apply pressure on the Greek colonists from the areas
they controlled in Campania. The Etruscan threat had
become even stronger when, at the start of the sixth
century, Etruria built up a powerful fleet. The Etruscans
were skillful seamen and, as such, rapidly established
themselves as the third strongest seapower of the
western basin of the Mediterranean, after the Greeks
and the Carthaginians. From then on, an endless
conflict pitted flourishing Greek cities such as Cumae,
Massalia (Marseilles), and Syracuse against the
maritime ambitions of the Etruscans.

In 560 B.C., the Greeks of Ionia founded Alalia, a new
colony in Corsica. When added to the existing Greek
colonies in Magna Graecia, Gaul, North Africa and even
on the Ligurian coast, this last city seemed to close the
circle that Greek sea power had built around Etruria. To
retain their access to the Tyrrhenian Sea, it was
essential for the Etruscans to loosen this grip, and at
any cost.

At the start of the sixth century, the Phoenician colony in Africa had also flourished, but its growth was likewise threatened and hindered by the Greeks. The Etruscans and Carthaginians therefore formed a coalition against their common enemy, the Greeks. Following numerous skirmishes, a decisive naval battle was fought at Alalia in 540.

Greek prisoners stoned to death

This is the first great sea battle to be documented by the writers of antiquity! The great Greek historian Herodotus relates:

"For five years the Greeks of Alalia annoyed their neighbors by plundering and pillaging on all sides, until at length the Carthaginians and Tyrrhenians leagued against them, and sent each a fleet of 60 ships to attack the town. The Greeks, on their part, manned all their vessels, sixty in number, and met their enemy on the Sardinian Sea. In the engagement which followed the Greeks were victorious, but their success cost them dearly. They lost 40 ships in the battle, and the 20 which remained came out of the engagement with beaks so bent and blunted as to be no longer serviceable. The Greeks therefore sailed back again to Alalia and, taking their wives and children on board, with such portion of their goods and chattels as the vessels could bear, bade adieu to Corsica and sailed to Rhegium.

"The Carthaginians and Tyrrhenians who had got into their hands many more than the Greeks from among the crews of the forty vessels that were destroyed, landed their captives upon the coast after the fight, and stoned them all to death." (1)

The Etruscans and Carthaginians thus claimed the final victory at Alalia. After the Greeks left Corsica, the Etruscans settled on the island and developed its natural ressources, including wax, honey, and wood.

By consolidating their alliance, the Etruscans and Carthaginians put an end to Greek hegemony on the Tyrrhenian coasts and restricted the Hellenic influence on the other western shores of the Mediterranean, which the victors shared. Whereas the Carthaginians claimed Sicily and Spain, the Etruscans established their rule in Latium and Campania.

The high point of Etruscan expansion

It was in the final third of the sixth century, after the victory over the Greeks in southern Italy and on sea, that Etruria decided to expand to the north.

Setting out this time from the northern lucumonies, the invaders burst into the Po Valley through the passes of the Tuscan Apennines. After gaining control of the native peoples, for the most part Umbrians, the Etruscans reached the Adriatic coast which they occupied as far as Pesaro.

In these newly conquered regions, the Etruscans built such cities as Melpum (Melpo), Verona, Piacenza, Cremona, Modena, Felsina (Bologna), and Ravenna. In their usual fashion, the Etruscan conquerors mingled

1. Histories of Herodotus, *Bk. I, 66 (p. 85)*.

with the earlier inhabitants, and brought their civilization and political institutions to the conquered lands. In
this way, as in Tuscany, the cities created in the Po
Valley and on the shores of the Adriatic formed a
dodecarchy (or federation of twelve cities) which
included Melpum, Piacenza, Cremona, Parma, Modena, Hatria, Spina, Ravenna, and Ariminum (Rimini).

By about 480 B.C., at the conclusion of their
northward expansion, Etruscan domination extended
across a substantial portion of modern Italy with the
exception of a few provinces—Piedmont, Liguria,
Puglia, Calabria—and some Greek colonies.

Etruscan power reached its zenith at the start of the
fifth century. In command of the major part of the Italian
peninsula, the basin of the Tyrrhenian Sea, and part of
the western Mediterranean, Etruria was the first nation
to achieve the unity of Italy. It was, however, only a
semblance of unity for, in the very heart of Italy, in
Latium, the Etruscan venture encountered increasing
opposition from the inhabitants of Rome, a city whose
name was soon to be engraved in gold in the annals of
world history.

Render unto Caesar what is Caesar's

The Etruscans had conquered Latium during the
advance south in 650 B.C. as noted above. They were to
remain its rulers until the end of the sixth century.

The Etruscan presence in Latium marked the
meeting of the two great civilizations of ancient
Italy—Etruria and Rome. The former was at the height

of its brilliance, while the latter was still in its infancy. But posterity remembers only the glorious name of Rome, relegating to oblivion the Etruscan civilization, which was older and, in some ways, richer in its contributions. This is probably so because Etruria was incapable of building a state; in contrast, Rome would excel at it.

"Render unto Caesar what is Caesar's." History scarcely heeded this advice in dealing with early Rome, a city which was actually *Etruscan*.

"It would astonish more than one mind stamped with a classical education," writes Alain Hus, "to be told that Rome was at first an Etruscan city and for more than a century, that was practically all it was. Our school memories, born of the one and only Roman tradition, have left us with an image of early Rome that is endearing but stereotyped: the twins, the wolf, and the famous seven kings. The assassination of Tarquinius Superbus (the Proud) is still for us the symbol of republican revolt against tyranny, a well-turned cliché invented by the Romans of the republic and piously transmitted from generation to generation. Even now we still consider the early history of Rome to be the history of a prestigious city. Not only is it difficult to imagine a Rome occupied by foreigners, it is also difficult to realize that it was also shaped and virtually founded by a foreign nation.

"And this foreigner was none other than Etruria . . . ."

Early Rome: A handful of small villages gathered together

What was Latium like in the middle of the seventh century, at the start of Etruscan expansion towards the south?

Inhabited by numerous tribes clustered in tiny villages—the largest of which never numbered more than a few thousand inhabitants—Latium had no political or ethnic unity. Nevertheless, to protect themselves against the imperialist goals of their powerful northern neighbors, these Latium villages formed defense leagues.

As it happens, Rome was located at one of the main gateways controlling access to Latium; hills and steep slopes on the left bank of the Tiber formed a natural barrier between Etruria and Latium. Latin outposts had long been established there to keep a watch on the movements of the Etruscans on the other side of the river. On the eve of the great Etruscan expansion towards the south, the Latin peoples who had settled on the heights of Rome formed a military and religious federation, the *Septimontium*, or federation of the seven hills, for protection against the foreign intruder.

Within this confederation, the members preserved a great deal of autonomy. In other words, at this early period in her history, Rome did not constitute a city, in the true sense of the word: (1) its name, *Septimontium*, referred only to a crude form of association without political unity or centralized power.

1. *The political concept of the* urbs *(city) had not yet made its appearance in Latium.*

"Towards the middle of the seventh century," writes the historian Léon Homo, "at the moment when the great Etruscan expansion was to begin, Latin civilization on Roman soil still remained rudimentary and poverty-stricken despite the advances noted above. The poor Roman villages, lost on the banks of the Tiber and sunk in their marshes, experienced foreign influence only to a slight degree. The currents of trade passed them by, and a few miles from the brilliant cities of southern Etruria—like Tarquinia, Veii, and Caere—the inhabitants of the Palatine, Esquiline and Quirinal continued to live as savages and primitives, whatever a partial tradition may say." (1)

Etruscan Rome

As an important crossroad on the way to rich Campania, Rome indeed occupied a vital position that the Etruscans, in their advance southward, were compelled to conquer. By the end of the seventh century, the Etruscans had seized the populated area of Latium: it has been historically established that until the end of the sixth century Rome was governed by three Etruscan kings—Tarquin the Elder, Servius Tullius, and Tarquin the Proud.

Roman history is full of gaps, however, unfortunately, apart from the Roman tradition as typified by Livy, few historical documents deal with this impor-

1. *Homo,* Primitive Italy and the Beginnings of Roman Imperialism, p. 98.

tant episode of Roman history. Admittedly, Roman tradition has been falsified on numerous points because the historians of the republic, out of nationalist pride, concealed the conquering aspect of the Etruscan presence. Nevertheless, under these Etruscan kings, Rome began the ascent that was to make it, a few centuries later, the capital of the world.

What does this Roman tradition tell us about these kings?

"In the course of the reign of the Roman king, Ancus," writes Livy, "a man named Lucumo left Tarquinia where he was born and came to settle in Rome. He was ambitious and wealthy and hoped to rise to a position of eminence there, such as his native town was never likely to afford him; for though born at Tarquinia he was by blood an alien, being the son of Demaratus of Corinth. Demaratus had been forced by political troubles to leave his country, and happened to settle in Tarquinia, where he married . . . .

"Lucumo, the sole heir of his father's property, had become in time as proud as he was wealthy, and his self-confidence had been further increased by his marriage to Tanaquil, an aristocratic young woman who was not the sort to put up with humbler circumstances in her married life than those she had previously been accustomed to.

"The Etruscans of Tarquinia had despised Lucumo as the son of foreign refugees, and to Tanaquil the indignity of his position had soon become intolerable; wholly bent upon seeing her husband enjoy the respect he deserved, she had smothered all feelings of natural affection for her native town and determined to abandon it forever. For the purpose she had in mind she had decided that the most suitable place was Rome; Rome was a young and rising community; there would be opportunities for an active and courageous man in a place where all advancement came swiftly and depended upon ability....

"Since the Roman king Ancus himself had had a Sabine mother.... Tanaquil had no difficulty in persuading her husband; he was already set upon improving his position, and the prospect of leaving Tarquinia—the birthplace of his mother only—caused him no distress."

Tanaquil, an expert in divination

"So they packed their belongings and left for Rome. The pair had reached Janiculum and were sitting together in their carriage, when an eagle dropped gently down and snatched off the cap which Lucumo was wearing. Up went the bird with a great noise of wings until, a minute later, it swooped down again and, as if it had been sent by heaven for that very purpose, neatly replaced the cap on Lucumo's head, and then vanished into the blue, Tanaquil like most Etruscans was well skilled in celestial prodigies, and joyfully accepted the omen. Flinging her arms around her husband's neck, she told him that no fortune was too high to hope for. 'Only consider,' she cried, 'from what quarter of the sky the eagle came, what god sent it as his messenger! Did it not declare its message by coming to your *head*—the highest part of you? Did it not take the crown, as it were, from a human head, only to restore it by heaven's approval, where it belongs?'

"Thus dreaming of future greatness, Lucumo and Tanaquil drove into Rome, where they bought a house, and Lucumo took the name of Lucius Tarquinius Priscus (the Elder). In Rome Lucumo soon began to attract attention as a wealthy stranger, and wasted no opportunity of advancing himself. Hospitable, free with his money, and always ready with a kindly word, he made friends rapidly, and it was not long before his reputation brought him to the palace.

"Once known to the king, he was quick to improve the acquaintance, serving him with such liberality and adroitness that he was soon admitted into intimacy and consulted upon every matter of private interest or national importance, both in peace and war, until he became indispensable and was even named in the king's will as guardian of his children." (1)

At the death of King Ancus in 616 B.C., the ambitious Tarquin was not content to act as tutor, the role assigned to him by the royal will and testament. He wanted to be king, to the detriment of the legitimate heir to the throne. At the meeting of the comitia for the election of a new king, therefore, he tried to win public support by speeches and harangues.

1. *Livy*, The Early History of Rome, *Bk. I, 33-35 (pp. 56-57).*

The work of the first Etruscan king in Rome

Tarquin the Elder was elected king by an over-
whelming majority and sought to consolidate his
power. He successfully warred against neighboring
Latin villages, thereby enlarging the territory of Rome.
To celebrate these military victories, Tarquin organized
games—horse races and boxing matches involving
mostly Etruscan athletes—which surpassed in magnificence all that Rome had ever known. The custom of
"Roman games" is thus Etruscan in origin.

Tarquin brought to Rome not only the customs of
his homeland but also the advanced economic techniques of the Etruscans.

"Tarquin the king set his people to various civic
undertaking with such enthusiasm," relates Livy, "that
they had even less leisure than they had had during the
wars. The building of the stone wall, interrupted by the
Sabine war, that was intended to protect those parts of
Rome which were as yet unfortified, was resumed; the
low-lying areas of the town around the Forum, and the
valleys between the hills, where flood-water usually
collected, were drained by sewers leading down into
the Tiber; and finally, the foundations of the temple of
Jupiter on the Capitol were laid. (1) During the Sabine
war, Tarquin had bound himself by a solemn vow to
build this temple: one cannot but feel that in some way
he already foresaw the future splendor of that famous
place" (Bk. I, 39; p. 61).

1. *This temple—the Capitol—was later decorated by artists from
Veii, the Etruscan city neighboring Rome.*

The power struggle in Rome

The reign of Tarquin the Elder lasted thirty-eight years, from 616 to 578 B.C.; it marked the beginning of an era of Etruscan royalty in Rome that did not end until the following century, with the republican revolution in 509.

This period of Roman history, marked by the domination of Etruscan kings, is described at length by Livy and many other Roman historians.

In 578 the first Tarquin was brutally murdered by a messenger hired by the sons of Ancus who had been denied their rightful claim to the throne. After his death the struggle for power in Rome became a conflict among the Tarquins themselves. According to Livy, Servius Tullius, the adopted son and son-in-law of Tarquin the Elder, expelled the latter's own sons in order to accede to the throne. Servius Tullius himself was later assassinated by one of the sons of Tarquin the Elder, who became king of Rome in 534 under the name Tarquinius Superbus (the Proud).

But numerous elements of this purely Roman version of the facts are contradicted by Etruscan tradition.

Indeed, official Roman history presents the struggle for power in Rome as an internal struggle, peculiar to Rome, marked by assassinations and treason. On the contrary, available Etruscan evidence (essentially the frescos of tombs) presents the history and fall of Etruscan Rome as but one episode of many in the interminable quarrels engaged in amongst themselves by the various expanding Etruscan cities. (1)

The Vulcians lay siege to Rome

These are the facts as they have been reassembled from Etruscan documents: In 578, Rome was besieged and conquered by the army of Vulci (a city of southern Etruria) under the command of Caelius Vibenna, assisted by his brother Aulus and his loyal lieutenant Mastarna. Caelius Vibenna managed to force the doors of the city but he was killed under obscure circumstances. Mastarna succeeded him.

The conquest of Rome by the Vulcians is abundantly illustrated in the paintings discovered in the François Tomb. One of the first scenes depicts Caelius Vibenna, naked and unarmed, a prisoner of Tarquin the Elder's soldiers. He is stretching out his bound hands to Mastarna who is cutting the ropes with his knife. A second panel shows three Vulcian warriors striking Roman prisoners. One of the victims is none other than *Tarchunies Rumach,* which in Etruscan signifies Tarquin of Rome or Tarquin the Elder.

The panel symbolizes an attempt by the Etruscan city of Vulci, which was at the height of its prosperity and military strength in the middle of the sixth century, to overcome its neighboring sister-cities, Tarquinia and Caere, and thus expand its territory.

1. *For the Etruscan version of these events, see particularly, the splendid ensemble of paintings in the François Tomb, discovered in Vulci in 1857.*

Polychrome terracotta statue of Apollo, life size, by the sculptor Vulca. From Veii. About 500 B.C. Villa Giulia Museum, Rome. *(Giraudon-Anderson)*

Terracotta statuette of a girl combing her hair. From Solaia, near Sart About 100 B.C. Florence Museum. *(Giraudon)*

Servius Tullius acceded to the throne

Was Servius Tullius, the man who succeeded Tarquin the Elder on the throne of Rome, actually the Vulcian lieutenant Mastarna, the companion of Caelius Vibenna? The Roman Emperor Claudius, who was the first to devote a lengthy study to the Etruscans (during the first century B.C.), categorically identified the two characters.

"According to Roman tradition," he wrote, "Servius Tullius was the son of a slave, Ocresia, and had been adopted by Tarquin the Elder and his wife Tanaquil; according to the Etruscans, he was Caelius Vibenna's loyal friend and companion during all his undertakings .... His Etruscan name was Mastarna, and it was after having changed his name that he seized the throne of Rome for the greater good of the Roman State." (1)

The reign of Servius Tullius, which lasted 44 years, was in fact a great boon to Rome. Roman historians themselves were later to recognize that he had been the greatest king and the greatest administrator of ancient Rome, and that, after Romulus, he was the city's second founding father.

Among Servius Tullius' most remarkable administrative accomplishments was the establishment of the census, the enumeration of Roman citizens according to their wealth.

1. *This text by the Emperor Claudius is quoted by Alain Hus,* Les Etrusques, peuple secret. *Many Latin historians have stated that Emperor Claudius, born in Lyons, had composed a monumental history of Etruria. Unfortunately, we possess only a few rare fragments of this lost work.*

"He originated the census," writes Livy, "a measure of the highest utility to a state destined, as Rome was, to future preeminence; for by means of it, public service, in peace as well as in war, could thenceforward be regularly organized on the basis of property; every man's contribution could be in proportion to his means" (Bk. I, 43; p. 65).

Another of his important works was the building of solid ramparts in order to protect Rome. Known as the Walls of Servius Tullius, numerous vestiges of them still exist today.

Tullia orders her chariot to drive over her father's corpse

Nevertheless, the reign of Servius Tullius was to have a tragic end.

In order to shield himself from the vengeance of Tarquin the Elder's two sons, the king had given them his two daughters in marriage. One of them, Tullia, was consumed by royal ambitions and repeatedly urged her husband, Lucius Tarquinius, to get rid of her own father Servius Tullius, whom she accused of usurping the throne.

"Come! Do your work!" Livy has her say. "You are no stranger, as your father was, from Corinth or Tarquinia. No need for you to struggle for a foreign throne; it is yours already; the guardian gods of your hearth and home proclaim you king! Your father's bust, his palace, his royal seat, his name and yours—in these is your title. You dare not? Then why continue to play the cheat? Why let men look on you as a prince?" (Bk. I, 47; p. 70).

Constantly provoked by Tullia against his father-in-law, Lucius Tarquinius—who was himself a hot-blooded, ambitious, and unscrupulous man—plotted the king's death. Since he did not dare sully his own hands with the blood of such a crime, he hired a handful of mercenaries to assassinate the king for a handsome fee. After the event, he proclaimed himself king in the name of his ancestors' legitimate right to the Roman throne.

Legend has passed on a particularly cruel anecdote concerning the death of Servius Tullius. His body lay abandoned by his assassins across the palace road when Tullia's chariot happened to pass by. When the driver saw the corpse, he stopped the horses, but Tullia ordered him to go on. The chariot wheels rolled over the body, breaking it into several sections. Tullia arrived home spattered by her father's blood!

Dictatorship and reign of terror

The reign of Lucius Tarquin, starting under such baneful circumstances, continued in tyrrany and terror. Because of his arrogant and supercilious attitude, the new king was soon dubbed "Tarquin the Proud."

Tarquin the Proud imposed his absolute, personal rule on Rome. In foreign affairs, decisions concerning war and peace, treaties and alliances were made at his whim, by the king's privy council or the king himself. The same tyranny prevailed in domestic matters.

According to the testimony of Roman historians, Rome had never known such a despot.

"He had usurped by force the throne to which he had no title whatever: the people had not elected him, the senate had not sanctioned his accession," writes Livy. "Without hope of his subjects' affection, he could rule only by fear; and to make himself feared as widely as possible he began the practice of trying capital cases without consultation and by his own sole authority. He was thus enabled to punish with death, exile, or confiscation of property not only such men as he happened to suspect or dislike, but also innocent people from whose conviction he had nothing to gain but their money" (Bk. I, 49; p. 72).

Rome under the harsh rule of the foreign invader

Such is the image offered to us, by the traditional Roman vew, of the last Etruscan king, Tarquin the Proud, a cruel, unscrupulous, and greedy tyrant who broke the law without hesitation in order to enrich himself. To present a view that is closer to historical fact, it is necessary to correct this image of the second Tarquin.

From an Etruscan point of view, Tarquin the Proud was merely imposing martial law on Rome, a city conquered by Etruscans. Under Tarquin the Proud, the Etruscan domination became more harsh and its methods more brutal. Tarquin initiated a system of genuine exploitation in Rome and the previously conquered areas of Latium, all the while striving to settle new Etruscan colonies in the province by way of continuous warfare.

Thus a truly Etruscan imperialist policy was being pursued to the detriment of the Romans. The two major aspects of this policy were, on the one hand, a vast construction program in Rome and, on the other, planned conquest of the unsubdued tribes of Latium. To reach these two goals, Tarquin did not hesitate to institute a reign of terror, tyranny, and violence.

The accomplishments of Tarquin the Proud

Pursuing the plans of his father, Tarquin the Elder, Tarquin the Proud completed the construction of the Temple of Jupiter on the Capitol. This temple, destined to immortalize the name of the Tarquins, was only the first objective of a vast urbanization program in Rome, and was soon followed by the construction of the circus and then the city's sewers.

Despite Livy's prejudice against Tarquin the Proud, tyrant and oppressor of the Roman people, the republican historian recognized the usefulness of the projects undertaken by this king.

"Tarquin's chief interest," he writes, "was now the completion of the temple. Builders and engineers were brought in from all over Etruria, and the project involved the use not only of public funds but also of a large number of laborers from the poorer classes. The work, hard in itself, came as an addition to their regular military duties, but because it was an honorable burden with a solemn and religious significance, they were not entirely unwilling to bear it. It was a very different matter when they were assigned to other tasks less spectacular but more laborious still, such as the construction of the tiers of seats in the circus and the excavation of the Cloaca Maxima, or Great Sewer, designed to carry off the sewage of the entire city by an underground pipe line. The magnitude of both of these projects could hardly be equalled by a work even of modern times" (Bk. I, 56; pp. 79-80).

While the urbanization of Rome was underway, Tarquin pursued a policy of conquest in order to consolidate and enlarge Etruscan possessions in Latium. His reign was involved in continual warfare—wars against the Volscians, against the Aequi, agains the Rutullians, all of whom rebelled against Etruscan influence. During these wars, the king proved to be a skillfull and courageous strategist. But Tarquin's accomplishments and warrior skills were finally incapable of altering the tragic course of Etruscan destiny.

For at this time, the end of the sixth century, serious political and military events brewing in Campania and in Latium foreshadowed the inescapable decline of the Etruscan empire.

Tarquin the Proud took flight

In 524 B.C., the Etruscans attempted to seize the Greek colony at Cumae in order to consolidate their position in Campania. Under the skillful command of their leader, Aristodemus, the Greeks drove back the attackers and inflicted a serious defeat upon them. The plan of the Greeks consisted in cutting the southern Etruscans off from their homeland by seizing the Etruscan territories of Latium and even Rome. To this end, they formed an alliance with the Latin tribes against the Etruscans.

In 509 B.C., word was brought to Tarquin in Ardea, where he had established camp in a war against the Rutullians, that disturbances had broken out in Rome. Accompanied by a small escort party, Tarquin galloped without delay to the city. When the king arrived the doors of the city were barred shut. A Roman messenger informed the king of his banishment and the Roman patricians' decision to seize power and abolish his dictatorship. The people and a part of the army had revolted....

"Rome is no place for a despot," the messenger repeated to Tarquin.

While Tarquin fled north to find refuge in Caere, his city of origin, the Roman Senate, in the presence of the assembled people, announced the fall of the Tarquins and proclaimed the republic.

Porsenna's counter-offensive

For Etruria, the expulsion of the Tarquins from Rome in 509 meant the loss of a key city of its empire. The city-states of Etruria could not accept such a disaster passively. Therefore, a short while after the flight of Tarquin the Proud, a counter-offensive against Rome was launched by Porsenna, king of Clusium. Following months of siege, a decisive battle took place at Aricia, twenty kilometers south of the Tiber. Despite its strength and the determination of Porsenna, its leader, the Etruscan army was unable to defeat the strong coalition of Romans and Latins, reinforced by Greeks from Cumae. The latter were the decisive factor in the Etruscan defeat, as witnessed by this passage from Livy:

"The engagement began with an Etruscan attack of such weight and fury that the Arician lines were completely disorganized; but the men of Cumae saved the day. Meeting force by strategy, they moved to the flank to allow the enemy to sweep past them, then turned and attacked them in the rear, with the result that the Etruscans were caught in a trap and cut to pieces almost in the moment of victory. Arruns (their leader) was killed, and a handful of Etruscan soldiers, having nowhere nearer to go, found their way to Rome, where they arrived unarmed and helpless and with no resource but to throw themselves on the Romans' mercy. They were kindly received and biletted in various houses. Some, when their wounds were healed, went home to tell their friends of the generous treatment they had received, but the majority of them were induced to stay in Rome by their growing affection for both the city and their hosts. They were allowed to live in a district which came to be known as the Tuscan Quarter" (Bk. II, 15; p. 105).(1)

The Etruscans had lost Rome forever.

---

1. *Now the* vicus Tuscus, *or street of the Etruscans, which runs from the Temple of Castor and Pollux in the Forum to the banks of the Tiber.*

The death knell of Etruscan power

After this major defeat in 506, the situation of the Etruscan empire became critical. Would Etruria be able to tip the scales in its favor, or had these successive defeats (at Cumae, Rome, Aricia) by the coalition of Rome (the Latins and the Greeks of Cumae) irrevocably tolled the death knell of Etruscan hegemony?

"The loss of Rome and Latium," Alain Hus writes, "was not in itself a disaster. But it was especially important as a symbol of Rome's destiny and the date at which this destiny began: the Etruscans had been definitely stopped in Campania and had reached the northern limits of their conquests. They were powerless to prevent the development of Greek sea power. The Etruscans were directly hit and were forced for the first time to give ground at the very doors of their homeland, at the junction point of two essential parts of their empire. The role played by the Greeks in this series of Etruscan failures was critical, and would continue to be so in the decades that followed. Nevertheless, it was Rome that struck the first blow at the very heart of Etruria, the first in a series which would prove to be fatal."

Once the Etruscans were driven from Rome and Latium, Rome came under the administration of a new caste of leaders, the patricians. Rome became a republic and gradually imposed its rule, first over Latium, then over the entire Italian peninsula, at the expense of Etruria, even though it was the Etruscans who had laid the foundations of Rome's urbanism and established its first administrative institutions.

From the fifth century to the end of the third century B.C., two principal factors thus dominated the history of the Italian peninsula: the withdrawal of Etruria until it was completely absorbed by the Roman State, and the irresistible rise of Rome.

A hundred years' war between Etruscans and Romans

Early in the fifth century the Latin peoples, protecting their recently recovered independence, allied themselves against Rome. In 499, a Roman victory over the Latins on Lake Regillius assured Rome's hegemony in Latium.

But, at the frontier of Latium, beyond the Tiber, the Etruscan threat to Rome remained serious. The struggle between Romans and Etruscans assumed the characteristics of a 100-year border war. Rome's principal enemy at this moment was a coalition of the powerful city-states of Veii, with territory covering the entire right bank of the Tiber, which acted as protector of the small neighboring cities.

In 485 Rome, attracted by Fidenae's location (north of Rome on the Tiber) and Latin population, attacked that city. Fidenae called upon its protector, Veii, for help against the Romans, whose fortune, after many long years of war, took a turn for the worse. The army of Veii advanced as far as Rome and occupied Janiculum. In 474, a 40-year truce was signed under conditions imposed by the victor, Veii.

Though Etruria managed to put a halt to Roman

expansion in 474, she suffered a second serious defeat—this time at the hands of the Greeks of Cumae. The Etruscan fleet was preparing to attack Cumae when a Hellenic navy appeared on the horizon to help the Cumaeans. These ships belonged to Syracuse, at the time the most powerful city of Magna Graecia. At Cumae, the Etruscan navy was crushed forever by the coalition of Cumaeans and Syracusans.

Etruria, forced to defend itself against both Rome and the Greeks, was also soon obliged to confront the Samnites, advancing from the Apennines. During the second half of the fifth century B.C., the Etruscans suffered failure after failure on all these fronts.

The rush of the mountain people for the plains

After the maritime defeat at Cumae, the Etruscans saw their territories in Campania threatened and pillaged by Samnite bands sweeping down from their hideaways in the central Apennines. Not only was Etruria threatened by the invasions of these Sabellian peoples, but so were the Roman and Greek territories.(1)

"Throughout the whole of southern and central Italy, the migrants were streaming down upon the plains and the coasts," writes Léon Homo. "The Sabellians, swooping down from their citadel in the Abruzzi, appeared and ultimately took root. The older

1. *The Sabellians were peoples of ancient Italy who lived in the central Apennines and the Adriatic watershed, such as the Sabines, Lucanians, Samnites, and Picenes.*

inhabitants, expelled or subdued, had to bow before the invaders; new states were founded. During the fifth century the political and the ethnographic maps of Italy were alike redrawn. The Sabellian peoples, young and overflowing with vigor, everywhere advanced. In the meanwhile Etruria, exhausted by her conquests and the resultant dispersion of her forces, and mortally wounded by the loss of Latium, was now reduced to the defensive, a position from which she was not destined to extricate herself." (1)

In 423, the Samnites were numerous and powerful enough to seize Capua, the Etruscan capital of Campania. The fall of Capua marked the end of the Etruscan presence in Campania and the loss of the most attractive portion of their empire.

The Fall of Veii

While the Etruscans of Campania were suffering Samnite invasions, the war between Veii and Rome resumed. As soon as their truce expired in 438, there began a bloody and indecisive struggle that was to last thirteen years. In 425, Fidenae was taken by the Romans and completely sacked. The conquered Veiians were forced to sign a 20-year truce.

During this period, Rome strengthened its southern border (against the Vulcians) and its eastern border (against the Sabines and the Aequi). In Etruria itself and unlike its rival, Veii had been weakened by an

1. *Homo,* Primitive Italy and the Beginnings of Roman Imperialism, *p. 138.*

attempt to open a route seaward that was blocked by another Etruscan city, Caere.

At the expiration of a second truce between Veii and Rome, the latter felt sufficiently strong not only to defeat the Veiians but also to seize their city. In 396, this glorious Etruscan city was systematically razed by the Romans and its inhabitants were massacred.

After the fall of Veii, the cities of southern Etruria dropped like ripe fruit into the hands of the Romans. This was the case with Capena, Nepi, and Sutri.

Long-haired, fair-skinned conquerors shouting wildly

At the beginning of the fourth century, defeated in the south, Etruria found itself threatened from the north by Gallic hordes that swept over the rich Po Valley after crossing the Alps.

On the very day of the fall of Veii to the Romans, the Etruscan garrison of Melpum, at the northern tip of the Etruscan empire in what is now Lombardy, crumbled under the assaults of Celtic bands.

Who were these Gauls who so suddenly appeared in Italy and who a few decades later would reach the very gates of Rome? The Gauls were Celtic in origin and therefore Indo-European and had been settled west of the Alps since the seventh century. Early in the fourth century, the expanding Gallic population was looking for new living space. They quickly selected the rich Po Valley, which this numerous and adventurous people thought to conquer without much difficulty.

In a period of 30 years the Gauls, "long-haired, fair-skinned conquerors shouting wildly," managed to conquer the entire northern territory of Etruria which then became Cisalpine Gaul.

Rome saved by the geese of the Capitol

The Gauls then marched southward for the express purpose of pillaging the prosperous cities of central Italy. According to Diodorus Siculus, thirty thousand Gauls crossed the Apennines in 391 and found themselves at the foot of the Roman fortifications of the Etruscan city of Clusium (Chiusi). After a few unsuccessful attemps to seize the fortified town by storm, they continued toward Rome.

At the sight of these invaders of an unknown race, panic overwhelmed the Romans and they fled in confusion. Only one group of soldiers remained, entrenching themselves in the fortress of the Capitol. Most of the city fell before the onslaught of the barbarians who looted, burned, and killed everything in their path. The siege of the Capitol lasted many months.

One night, the Gauls made an attempt to avail themselves of the darkness and seize the fortress. The besiegers silently climbed to the top of the hill while the Roman sentinals slept soundly. According to Livy, Juno's sacred geese, spared despite the famine, sounded the alarm.

Rome was saved. Both sides were exhausted by this long siege and decided to negotiate a treaty: Rome bought its freedom for a thousand pounds of gold and the Gauls departed.

Caere became a Roman city

The war against the Gauls had considerably weakened Rome. Fire had completely devastated the city. The time seemed propitious for the powerful Etruscan metropolis of Tarquinia. She formed a coalition with the peoples neighboring Rome in an attempt to destroy the capital of Latium. But once again Etruria was incapable of uniting itself. Instead of fighting at the side of its fellow countrymen, Caere, though directly threatened, allied itself with Rome. Tarquinia's attempt ended in defeat in 382.

Twenty-four years later, in 358, Tarquinia formed a new alliance, this time with Caere and the Faliscans.(1) The ensuing seven years of warfare ended disastrously for the Etruscans in 351.

When Tarquinia signed a truce with the victors, the peace terms imposed upon Caere by the Romans were extremely harsh: the city was placed under Roman administration and forced to pay a sizable tribute. This ancient Etruscan city became a Roman city.

For the next 50 years, the Etruscans passively witnessed Roman expansion in every direction: in Campania, in Puglia, and on the shores of the Adriatic.

1. *An Italic tribe which had settled between Etruria and the Roman territory west of the middle Tiber. Its capital was Falerii Veteres (the present-day Civita Castellana).*

A daring maneuver by the Roman general Rullianus

In 312 B.C., the Samnites, who had driven the Etruscans and Greeks from Campania and had been fighting Rome for 15 years, finally joined forces with the the Etruscans. At this time all Italic peoples were faced with a crucial choice : submit entirely to Roman rule, or unite in a vast coalition against the Roman ambition for hegemony. The Samnites, Etruscans, Umbrians, Gauls, and others soon created a league, and their war against Rome lasted nearly 33 years, from 312 to 280 B.C.

The first setback occurred on the Etruscan front. In 310, for the first time, the allies of Etruria brought their combined forces to bear against Sutri—gateway to Etruria—which was held by the Romans. While Roman forces in the town square of Sutri were resisting Etruscan attacks, the Roman general Rullianus attempted a daring maneuver. Leading his army, he went deep into the Cimine forest and emerged in the very heart of Etruria by way of an unexpected and supposedly impassable road. The Etruscans hurriedly regrouped the army, but were slaughtered by the Romans at Perugia. This first phase of the war ended in 308 with the submission of central Etruria. Tarquinia was forced to surrender part of her territory to Rome.

The end of the resistance against Rome

A few years later, the Italic coalition determined to strike another major blow. The Etruscans and the Gauls brought the war as far as the banks of the Tiber while the Umbrians, Sabines, and Samnites provoked innumerable other battles. However, Roman strategy and daring once again succeeded in overcoming the inchoate, though courageous efforts of the Italic peoples.

The coalitionists then suffered a new series of defeats: the Etruscans at Volterra, the Gauls and Samnites at Sentinum in 295. Central Etruria was definitely under control of the Roman sphere of incluence.

The struggle of the Italian peoples continued sporadically for a short while longer. But gradually, one after another, the rebel tribes laid down their arms or withdrew from the coalition, as the Gauls did in 283. The last bastions of the Etruscan struggle, the city-states of Vulci and Volsinii, signed a peace treaty with Rome in 280; they were forced to surrender a large portion of their territory.

Rome was the great victor. After nearly 100 years of warfare against the many peoples of the Italian peninsula, Rome had forever established its rule over all of central Italy .... Numbers provide the most precise and most eloquent commentary on the work that had been accomplished. Midway through the fourth century, before the Italian peoples had massively waged war against Rome, the Roman state covered approximately 4,250 square miles; in 280 it stretched over an area of 31,660 square miles, three-fourths of the Italian peninsula.

Two thousand statues as booty

At the end of the wars of independence, Volsinii was the one active member of the Italian league against Rome to maintain its independence, though diminished in size. Well protected by its fortified ramparts, the prosperous Etruscan metropolis stood in defiance of Roman power.

In 265, troubles in Volsinii provided Rome with the opportunity to forcibly seize this Etruscan citadel. Indeed, a popular rebellion had brought former slaves to power and Volsinii was stricken with plebeian violence and anarchy .... Volsinian aristocrats, determined to take back the power they had been stripped of, appealed to the Romans for help. But the Romans symbolically reinstated the aristocrats merely to mask their true objective, which was to reduce the Etruscan city to slavery. They exploited Volsinii and deported its inhabitants. Pillage of the city yielded 2,000 statues and a large number of very valuable works of art.

The fall of Volsinii in the year 265 marks the final defeat of Etruria, an end which clearly reveals the deep-seated causes of Etruria's decline and disappearance: constant dissension among the Etruscan cities and even within each city, social dissension that Rome's opportunistic policy was able to exploit admirably.

All roads lead to Rome

What was the nature of ancient Etruria after its integration into the Roman republic? Like the other conquered regions of the peninsula, Etruria underwent a process of Romanization.

Romanization, or the assimilation of conquered peoples, was neither a rapid nor a brutal process. But while Rome did grant these subdued cities their freedom of religion and way of life, it subjected them to an inflexible government.

Close to the native cities, Rome founded numerous colonies inhabited by Romans. To facilitate communications between these colonies and the other cities, on the one hand, and between the capital and all the conquered territories, on the other, an astounding network of roads was built, all of which, according to the proverb, led to Rome. This network of roads, the "Roman ways," constituted one of Rome's most lasting works.

Notable among the Roman colonies in Etruria were Cosa, near Vulci, and even Alsium and Fregenae. The Roman roads were particularly numerous in Etruria. Among them were the *Via Aurelia* from Rome to Pisa, and the *Via Cassia* from Rome to Florence, passing through Veii, Volsinii, Clusium, and Arretium.

Thanks to the constant exchanges with the Roman colonies, the "autonomous" cities of the Roman Empire gradually patterned themselves after the Roman capital. In Etruria as well as in other conquered provinces, the Pax Romana set in to last for many centuries.

About the middle of the third century, Etruria disappeared politically, but it survived through its meticulous rituals and superstitions. In Rome itself, Etruscan priests continued to practice their art. Major

Roman events were held according to the prophecies and premonitions of Etruscan diviners. Vanquished Etruria held in its hand a powerful and secret instrument of revenge against the city that had conquered it, Rome.

Although Etruscan art, customs, and religion survived and permeated many aspects of life in both the Roman republic and the Empire, Roman historians were not inclined to glorify the memory of Etruria, and this admirable civilization sank into oblivion.

3

MAGI, PRIESTS, AND DIVINERS: ETRUSCAN RELIGION

"A predilection for magic and concern with the here-after were more than enough to give Etruscan religion the somber character of which all Etruria's rites and monuments bear the traces."

A. Bouché-Leclercq
Histoire de la divination

Despite the vast number of tombs and funerary monuments on Etruscan soil that were brought to light a long time ago, despite the numerous texts handed down to us by Greek and Roman historians, the study of Etruscan civilization still encounters many gaps and mysteries. The puzzling religion of the Tuscans arouses as many heated controversies and theories as do the origins of this mysterious people.

A religion with no legible texts

In his very recent and monumental study noted above, Georges Dumézil emphasizes that the exceptional wealth of funerary material does not give us any precise knowledge about Etruscan theology.

"Finally, despite a considerable body of work, Etruscan religion remains obscure. When we speak of it, we are obliged to dwell on its best-known aspects, notably the various forms of divination which were of particular interest to the officials and the scholars of Rome. But this emphasis certainly unbalances our survey, at the expense of theology, the most important element of any religion, and at the expense of the calendar festivals, of which we are almost wholly ignorant. It is a risky business to try to describe the religion of a people whose texts are incomprehensible."(1)

Dumézil than alludes to the many cities of the Etruscan confederation and the diverse nature of Etruscan religion—with each city having its own system of beliefs—and adds that archeological excavations of Etruscan tombs provide no clear indications of the religious rites practiced in one place or another in Etruria.

Obscure, hermetic, incomprehensible divinities

Massimo Pallottino, the great Italian Etruscologist, shares this opinion; after forty years of research devoted to sanctuaries, temples, funerary monuments, and inscriptions, he concludes that the interpretation of Etruscan religion is still a very difficult undertaking.

1. *Georges Dumézil,* Archaic Roman Religion, *p. 626.*

Neither he nor the large archeological team under his direction, who have been endeavoring to decipher the inscriptions and paintings found in the tombs of ancient Etruria, have yet succeeded in determining whether Etruscan religion, fatalistic and dominated by obscure, incomprehensible divinities, suggested precise ethical principles to the Etruscan believer.

To be sure, they have demonstrated—as we will see later—that both the private and public lives of the Etruscans were totally governed by religion. But there is no proof that this religious practice was based on clearly defined metaphysical and moral grounds.

The Etruscan triads

Faced by the difficulties that arise from the intrinsic study of this strange religion, some authors have sought a solution by adopting what Georges Dumézil calls the "comparative method." Since Etruscan religion itself resists any approach by way of synthesis, why not analyze some of its elements in order to compare and contrast them with those of other religions?

Georges Dumézil himself devoted a great deal of research to the supreme triad of the Etruscan pantheon (Tinia-Uni-Menrva) and, basing his argument on sound archeological evidence, asserts that this triad reflects the partly Indo-European nature of Tuscan religion:

"There is no religion which does not impose an order, a more or less rigid, more or less coherent, more or less complete structure upon the bulk of its representations, particularly of its gods. The Etruscans cannot have been an exception to this rule . . . . Even if the excavations prove the theory that the Etruscans had a particular taste . . . . for temples with three *cellae* [chapels], and thus for combinations of three gods, this does not prove that the three gods were invariably these three, or the same ones." (1)

Parallels between the Etruscans and Chaldeans

As we have already mentioned, other Etruscologists, notably the supporters of the oriental origin of the Etruscans, have endeavored to find the sources of Tuscan religion in Asia Minor. The discovery in 1877 of the famous Piacenza liver provided the opportunity to conduct a comparative study of hepatomancy [divination from the liver] and gave substance to such research. The connection between this Etruscan liver and the numerous livers discovered in Anatolia and Mesopotamia (discussed in the first chapter of this book) appears highly plausible. Jean Nougayrol notes accordingly that the gall bladder on the Chaldean liver found at Mari bears five lines of inscriptions, the fourth of which seems to mean "and the rain in the enemy country." Now, according to Pliny, Etruscan haruspices believed that the gall bladder was governed by Neptune, the rain god. The Piacenza liver also has five inscribed sections, the second of which bears the letter N, which may be interpreted as Neptune's initial. In a well-documented article, Jean Nougayrol mentions

1. *Georges Dumézil,* Archaic Roman Religion, *pp. 684-85.*

many other parallels between the Piacenza liver and the livers of Asia Minor. According to him, Etruria continued the haruspical traditions of Mesopotomia, and the analogies between Etruscans and Babylonians could not possibly have been accidental.

"Assyro-Babylonian haruspicy," concludes Jean Nougayrol, "is a continuous tradition which is revealed to us, already fully armed, on the verge of the second millennium B.C., and which follows its course, augmented by all kinds of subtle commentaries or critical apparatuses, down to the eve of our own era. The finest hepatoscopic tablets of the Louvre date from the ninetieth to the hundredth year of the Seleucid epoch.... Rough models and anatomical sketches from the Sargonid period have likewise come down to us.... In other words, the Etruscan models, wherever one locates them, will always find contemporaries in the East." (1)

The god Tin, a nude youth holding a thunderbolt in his hand

The Italian Etruscologist Pallottino sharply criticizes this theory. As we noted earlier, he believes the Etruscans to be the original inhabitants of Etruria, natives who could only have been influenced by peoples living near their territory or involved in prolonged trade relations with them. Etruria's closest

1. *Jean Nougayrol, "Haruspicine étrusque et assyro-babylonienne,"* Comptes rendus de l'Académie des Inscriptions et Belles Lettres *(1955), pp. 510-511, as quoted in Dumézil, p. 657.*

neighbors, main clients, and suppliers were of course the Greek colonists who had long been settled in the south of Italy. Therefore light can be shed on the mysteries of the Etruscan religion by comparing it with Greek beliefs. Pallottino substantiates this claim by outlining the relationship between the Etruscan pantheon and the Greek pantheon. His demonstration, it must be acknowledged, is convincing.

According to this author, the Greeks provided the Etruscans with the majority of their divinities. Thus, some of the features of the Etruscan gods Letha, Laran, and Maris were adapted from the Greek god Ares. This viewpoint, however, does not exclude the possibility of some oriental influence, apparent in the case of a few Etruscan warrior divinities such as the god Tin. In numerous frescoes decorating the tombs of Tarquinia, Caere and Vulci, bronze statuettes represent Tin as a nude youth holding a thunderbolt in his hand. But these oriental influences appear only rarely in the Etruscan pantheon.

Pallottino goes on to cite numerous examples of Greek gods worshipped in Etruscan cities early in their history. In adopting the Greek pantheon, the Etruscans did not even feel the need to modify it.

"A number of Greek divinities were also introduced directly into Etruria: Herakles, who became the Hercle of the Etruscans and the Hercules of the Romans; Apollo, who in Etruria became Apulu or Aplu; Artemis, known as Aritimi or Artumes. Characteristic specializations of gods, myths, and ritual also gradually came to be modelled upon corresponding Greek forms.... Monuments and texts give evidence of the variety and complex origin of the Etruscan pantheon." (1)

The tablets of Pyrgi : a new puzzle

A recent archeological discovery, however, has further complicated the study of Etruscan religious sources: the discovery in 1963 of tablets bearing Etruscan and Punic inscriptions in the sanctuary of Pyrgi, one of the ports of Caere. These tablets have been dated by means of Carbon-14 measurement, and apparently hark back to the beginning of the fifth century B.C.

The French epigraphical expert André Dupont-Sommer, who studied this exceptional document, has translated the Punic portion of these inscriptions as follows :

"To the Lady Astarte.

"This sacred place, it is what has been made and what has been given by Tebarie Velianas, king of Caere in the month of the sacrifice to the Sun, as his (own) gift, comprising the temple and its high place, because Astarte has favored her faithful one : in the year 3 of his reign, in the month of KRR, on the day of the Burial of the Goddess.

"And may the years in which the statue of the Goddess will reside in her temple be years as numerous as those stars yonder." (2)

1. *Massimo Pallottino,* The Etruscans, *p. 142.*
2. *André Dupont-Sommer, "L'inscription punique récemment*

The author then deals with the Etruscan portion of the inscription. Though he is unable to translate it—the Etruscan language is still inaccessible—he does identify the names of the donor, Tebarius Velianas, and of the Etruscan goddess Uni, or Juno. He reminds us that a work by Saint Augustine states that Juno is called Astarte in Punic *("lingua punica, Juno Astarti vocatur")*.

A detailed analysis of these tablets leads Dupont-Sommer to divulge several traits common to Etruscan and Punic rites, celebrations and calendars. He also observes that oriental cults in general, and the Phoenician cult in particular, exerted a "strange fascination" on the Etruscans.

A flexible theology, open to all foreign influences

What are we to think of all these theories? Was Etruscan religion Greek, Chaldean, or Semitic?

According to the great historian Albert Grenier, it sprang from a fusion of numerous elements from both the distant Anatolian plains and the nearby Greek colonies in southern Italy. Etruscan theology was a flexible theology, open to the whole range of foreign influences. Grenier reminds us also that the Etruscan people were sailors and tradesmen, in constant and prolonged contact with the many civilizations flourishing on the Mediterranean seaboard.

In a long and brilliant demonstration, the author

découverte à Pyrgi (Italie)," Journal asiatique *(March 1964), as quoted* in Dumézil, p. 680.

skillfully depicts these tireless voyagers, the Etruscans, traveling through a wide variety of countries, casting anchor at the farthest ports of the Mediterranean, exchanging goods, raw materials and religious ideas. (1)

"The antecedents of Etruscan religion," Albert Grenier concludes, "are to be found in the Asiatic religions of around 1,000 B.C. or earlier. Now, the recent discovery of Asiatic documents of the second millennium before our era, such as the tablets of Boghaz Keui and Ras-Shamra, have contributed and will continue to contribute much information on the religions and cults of early Asia." (2)

The historian Theopompus, "antiquity's worst gossip"

To sum up, such is the controversy over the sources of Etruscan religion, which continues to arouse heated debates among Etruscologists as noted earlier.

What did this religion consist of?

What practices did this religion impose upon "one of the most devout and most learned people in religious

1. *For a magnificent portrayal of the commercial dynamism of the Etruscans, ee the article by François Villard entitled "Chronologie du commerce étrusque d'exportation," published in the Belgian review* Latomus *(1962). The author provides precise figures on Etruria's volume of commercial exchanges with the countries on the western Mediterranean, particularly with the south of France.*
2. *Albert Grenier,* Les Religions étrusques et romaines, *"Mana" collection (Introduction to the History of Religions. (Paris : Presses universitaires de France, 1948.)*

matters, the religion experts of Rome," as Dumézil has
phrased it? (1) These enigmatic and admirable Etruscan necropolises in their frozen solitude, whose
vestiges have turned up along the banks of the Tiber
and the Arno and over the breathtaking landscapes
of Florence—to what divine messages do they tes-
tify?

As we have noted, two sets of sources provide
information on Etruscan theology: archeological
remains (tombs, temples, sanctuaries, and funeral
inscriptions of all kinds), and literary documents
handed down by Greek and Roman historians.

Some of these historians have minimized the
Etruscan heritage, out of national pride. (Rome was
scarcely, or not at all, indebted to Etruscan civilization,
assert many historians of the Roman Republic.) Others
have yielded to a predilection for systematic disparage-
ment, such as the historian Theopompus, whom Paul
Frischauer, Viennese archeologist and professor of the
history of ancient civilization, believes to have been a
"horrible gossip with the most malicious tongue in
antiquity." (2)

1. *Georges Dumézil,* L'Héritage indo-européen à Rome, *3rd edition,
collection "La Montagne Sainte-Geneviève" (Paris: Gallimard, 1949).
This book, part of a series under Dumézil's general editorship, is
more or less an early outline of the author's recently published
monumental work,* Archaic Roman Religion, *which has been cited
earlier. Though both books are fascinating from cover to cover,
neither one succeeds in providing the definitive answer to the crucial
question of the origins of Rome, origins as mysterious as those of
the Etruscans.*
2. *Paul Frischauer,* Archéologie de la sexualité *(Paris: Stock, 1969).
In this book the author devotes a very fine chapter to Etruscan
mores.*

On the other hand, authors such as Pliny, Seneca, Livy, Aulus-Gellius, and Cicero, attempted to restore the religious heritage of the Etruscans, although in doing so they sometimes exhibited certain prejudices.

The god Tages: a child endowed with the wisdom of old age

The most striking feature of Etruscan religion is that, unlike Greek and Latin religions, it was based on a revelation. Two prophets, one male, Tages, and the other female, Vegoie (also called Begoë or Bigois), had revealed to the Etruscans their basic religious rules and rituals.

Cicero, the author of the famous *De Divinatione*, is responsible for handing down the tale of Tages' appearance in the form of a boy endowed with the wisdom of old age. To validate his narrative somewhat, the famous Roman orator asserts that he has obtained his story from a very ancient Etruscan tradition:

"The tradition is that, once upon a time, in the district of Tarquinia, while a field was being plowed, the plowshare went deeper than usual and a certain Tages suddenly sprang forth and spoke to the plowman. Now this Tages, according to the Etruscan annals, is said to have had the appearance of a boy, but the wisdom of a seer. Astounded and much frightened at the sight, the rustic raised a great cry; a crowd gathered and, indeed, in a short time, the whole of Etruria assembled at the spot. Tages then spoke at length to his numerous listeners, who received with eagerness all that he had to say, and committed it to writing. His whole address was devoted to an exposition of the science of soothsaying." (1)

The curses of Vegoie against the movers of boundary markers

The second part of the Etruscan revelation came from Vegoie, who taught her people how to interpret lightning and gave them precise rites for setting the boundaries of fields, territories, and cities. The pragmatism of this latter instruction bears close ressemblance to the teachings of the Koran, where concern for a believer's daily life plays a greater role than theological subtleties. The *Liber Vegoie*, a collection of the goddess Vegoie's utterances, has unfortunately not survived. The Etruscan-born Roman historian Tarquitius Priscus (1st century) did record a few fragments, however.

The most important and most revealing fragment with respect to Etruscan religious sensibility is titled *Excerpt from the Book of Vegoie to Arruns Velthumnus* (Arruns was the king of Clusium, the present-day Chiusi):

"Be it known that the sea was separated from the sky. Whereas, when Jupiter had claimed the land of Etruria, he decreed and ordered that the plains be

1. *Cicero,* De Senectute, De Amicitia, De Divinatione, *trans. William Armistead Falconer (Cambridge: Harvard University Press, 1927), Bk. II, xxiii, 50 (p. 429).*

measured and that limits be set for the fields. Mindful of human greed and the passions aroused by land ownership, he wanted everything to be defined by boundary markers. When someone, some day, driven by the avarice of the end of the eighth century, will look upon the property that has been granted to him with contempt and covet the property of others, these markers will be violated, tampered with, and displaced by the fraudulent schemes of men. But whosoever touches them or moves them to enlarge his own property and diminish that of others will be condemned by the gods for this crime. If they are slaves, they will fall into deeper bondage. But if there is collusion by the master, his house will be destroyed and his entire family shall perish. Dire illness and injury will plague those who displace boundary markers and their sickly limbs shall be stricken. Storms will often shake the earth or tornadoes will make it tremble. Crops will frequently be spoiled and flattened by rain and hail, and they will perish by heat and drought, and be destroyed by rust. There will be civil strife. Be it known that such punishments will be brought to pass when these crimes occur. Therefore be not of bad faith nor of deceitful tongue. Abide by our teachings." (1)

1. *Text was included in the admirable work by G. A. Mansuelli,* Les Etrusques et les commencements de Rome, *"L'Art dans le monde" collection, monographs on great civilizations (Paris: Albin Michel, 1965). It is one of the best introductory works about the Etruscans, especially good on their artistic genius.*

The foundation of Rome according to Etruscan rites

Vegoie, the tutelary divinity of landed property, must have been held in great esteem by a people consisting almost entirely of peasants deeply attached to their plots of land. But the Etruscans were also builders and city-dwellers, "a people who," according to the Roman architect and author Vitruvius, "acquired great skill in building cities, of which many beautiful examples may be found in Etruria." And the founding of cities is specifically included among the rules and rituals recorded in the *Liber Vegoie*.

Basing his account on the historian Plutarch, the poet Ovid, and the architect Vitruvius, Albert Grenier tells the story of Rome's foundation (whose origins we now know were many), according to Etruscan rites handed down by Vegoie.

"When Romulus wanted to found Rome," writes Grenier, "according to Plutarch he began by calling in specialists from Etruria to teach him the proper rites and expressions. This had nothing to do with physical orientation, although some have claimed they recognize an Etruscan layout in the remains of the oldest substructures of the Forum; today this is debatable. Plutarch mentions only the digging of a pit, the *mundus*, where the *Comitium* was later located, into which the first fruits 'of all good things' were thrown and on top of which each new citizen came to deposit a bit of earth from the region of his birth. Ovid informs us that the pit was probably filled in and an altar erected over it where the hearth of the future city was to

burn. Then came the ceremony for tracing the city walls
with a bronze-bladed plow yoked to a bull and a cow.
Romulus' kin followed behind him, taking care to throw
all clods of earth back into the furrow; this was the
primordial furrow bordering the *pomoerium* which no
one was allcwed to cross. Because of this the city's
founded took care to lift the plow in order to interrupt
the furrow at the place where gates had been planned.

"In the typical Etruscan town, according to the
traditional prescriptions, there were to be three gates
located at the end of the town's two major arteries, with
the northern end of the *cardo* blocked off by the
acropolis. Referring to Etruscan ways, Vitruvius states
that the gods were supposed to be able to see most of
the city and its walls at a glance from the summit of this
acropolis where the temples were erected."

"The dark green cucumber and the pot-belly gourd"

Who were these gods that supposedly could take in
the city in one glance? How many of them were there?
There were three of them, like the three gates of Rome:
Tinia, Uni, and Menrva-Menerva, who were later
superseded by Jupiter, Juno, and Minerva. They
constituted the supreme triad, at the summit of the
Etruscan pantheon after the prophet-founders Tages
and Vegoie.

Tinia held a dominant position similar to the role of
Jupiter in Rome and Zeus in Greece. His symbol was the
thunderbolt, a basic element, as we will see later, of

Etruscan augury and a symbol of divine power and will. Tinia possessed three thunderbolts whereas most of the other gods had but one. As for Uni, she perpetuated the role of Vegoie, since she was believed to be the protectress of cities. According to Livy, transferring the statue of Uni from the conquered city of Veii to Rome was a major event. Uni enjoyed widespread popularity and was described as "the adorable nymph," "the delight of the Etruscan genre," "the heroic mistress" and by other equally laudatory metaphors. Menerva or Minerva was often depicted on vases or the walls of Etruscan tombs as a warrior goddess armed from head to foot, with a figure of Victory hovering above her head.

Aside from the divinities of the supreme triad, undoubtedly the most important god was Vertumnus (also Voltumna or Veltha). All Etruscan iconographic documents depict Vertumnus coming immediately after one of the three supreme deities. (1) Considered to be a major Etruscan god *(Deus Etruriae princeps)* by certain Latin authors, he appears to have come from Volsinii. Painted as a beardless, muscular, and strong young man, he presided over the creative forces of the universe. He was the god of the vegetable world, of "the dark green cucumber and the pot-belly gourd." Moreover, this is the way he describes himself in the famous elegy by the Latin poet Propertius:

1. *We have gathered and summarized this material from Mansuelli's excellent work* Les Etrusques et les commencements de Rome, *cited above.*

Tuscus ego, et Tuscus orior

I am the god Vertumnus;
place of birth: Etruria,
nationality of parents: Etruscan
The origin of my name: . . . the first fruits of the year
are offered to me as season follows season . . . .·
It's my name, so I ought to know.
And anyway I'm a god.
I've a natural talent as an impersonator:
you choose the part, I'll play it to perfection . . . .
—that's the one thing about me that goes without
[saying:
people offer to me the pick of their gardens.
My trademark is the dark green cucumber,
the pot-belly gourd . . . .
And every flower that opens its mouth in the
[meadow
looks lovely wilting on my brow . . . . (1)

Etruria with innumerable local cults

It would not be worthwhile to draw up an exhaustive list of all the Etruscan gods. Their number, their functions, their graphic representations, and even their names changed from city to city. We have already mentioned that ancient Etruria did not constitute a nation in the true sense of the word, but was a

1. The Poems of Propertius, *trans. John Warden (Indianapolis: Bobbs-Merrill, 1972), Bk. IV, 2 (pp. 195-196).*

confederation of twelve city-states (a figure still open to
debate among historians). These cities were posses-
sive of their independence, their institutions and, of
course, their gods.

There were numerous temples to Vertumnus in
Volsinii but his cult was almost insignificant in
Populonia which, on the other hand, dedicated its
most beautiful sanctuaries to Phuphluns, god of wine
and Bacchic orgies. Maris, the god of war and
agriculture, was honored in Vulci but ignored in Veii.
Turms was venerated in Arretium but his name was
apparently unknown in Tarquinia, although the latter
had been the "capital" of Etruscan religion. Sethlans,
god of fire and underground forges, was the guardian
spirit of Perusia: vestiges of a large temple erected
in his name are still standing near the city. But no
traces of this god can be found in cities such as Chiusi,
Vetulonia, and Marzabotto, where the gods Aplu
(Apollo) and Hercle (Hercules) enjoyed widespread
popularity.

We have also found traces of many female divinities
such as Tiv, goddess of the moon; Artumes (Artemis),
often depicted on mirrors with her brother Apollo;
Turan, mother-goddess, guardian of women and love,
animals, life and death. Turan is often represented
in paintings as a young woman dressed only to the
waist or completely nude. Is she Hera? Aphrodite?
Persephone? Or rather is she a synthesis of all
these divinities with various features drawn from
each?

Remains which still puzzle archeologists

As in many other areas of Etruscology, we know very little about the Etruscans' metaphysical outlook. To be sure, one need only travel in present-day Tuscany, view the vast necropolises and contemplate their variously shaped tombs to realize that the Etruscans were deeply preoccupied by the question of death. The prodigious funerary luxury encountered in all these tombs is testimony to this obsession. But we do not know what form this preoccupation took, nor do we know for sure the precise significance of this wealth.

These splendid paintings, vases, statues, everyday objects filling the depths of necropolises—are they evidence that the Etruscans envisioned a life after death or do they mean something else? Here, once again, the impenetrable silence of the Tuscan language leaves us face to face with many articles whose meaning escapes us completely. Albert Grenier writes:

"The most significant documents are the paintings which decorate the walls of the funeral chambers. But their interpretation raises a number of problems. Consider, for example, during the archaic era (sixth and fifth centuries), the scenes of the hunt or of returns from the hunt. How are they related to life beyond the grave? Are they the expression of hopes for the other life or the representation of memories dear to the deceased, or, even more simply, a decoration of the grave analogous to that in the richest dwellings of the living? Do the monsters of earth and sea portayed there inhabit the underworld or are they only decorative motifs borrowed from Greek art? Do the scenes of banquets, dances, music, and games of every kind take place in the nether world or on earth? Are they something other than the representation of the ceremonies which accompanied the funeral rites? Are they intended to prolong the benefit of those ceremonies for the dead person, for as long as the paintings shall last?... Later, starting with the fourth century, the scenes on the walls of the graves are localized in the underworld, but their meaning is not always clear." (1)

"They hesitated near the urn, their glances fixed"

This abundance of documents, as we can see, does not eliminate uncertainty. It is widely believed that the Etruscans, who as a general rule practiced inhumation, first believed that their dead continued to live in their own graves, which explains the richness of these monuments, some of them architectural masterpieces. The admirable necropolises of Volterra, for example, which were obviously intended for the city's aristocratic elite, inspired the great Italian poet, Gabriele D'Annunzio, to write some of his most beautiful pages. Of courses, the author of the moving *Martyrdom of Saint Sebastian* was not an archeologist versed in the art of making stones speak. But his poetic sensibility restored the tragic, melancholy mood that still pervades the funeral ruins of Tuscany. These ruins, D'Annunzio suggests, are testimony to the Etruscans'

1. *Albert Grenier,* La Religion étrusque, *pp. 54-55, as quoted in* Dumézil, Archaic Roman Religion, *p. 691.*

belief in the hereafter, the belief that death was not the absolute end of life, but rather another form of life.

One of the famous passages of D'Annunzio's *La Città Morta*, a drama set in Volterra in what was formerly Etruria, occurs when the two young heroes Paolo and Vana, visit the city's museum to find "the eternal longing of their souls":

" ... with cautious eyes they discovered indications of their own destiny everywhere, manifest images of their most secret thoughts ....

" 'What great silence to be in such small rooms,' the brother said. 'He who leaves does not weep, he who remains does not weep.'

"They stared fixedly at each other, hand in hand, bidding farewell without words, near the back of the sepulcher. and the winged witness was none other than the divine Sadness. For Sadness is the Etruscan muse. It is she who accompanied along the roads of exile and hell the great Etruscan colored by black bile .... The *Manes* (souls of the dead), on foot and on horse, rode before those travelers moving in covered caravans, litters, triumphal chariots. The harnessed coursers bent low their collars so their manes touched the ground in the manner of Achilles' Alezan, presaging death ....

" 'Is this not a picture of me? asked the brother, stopping before it. Of all the routes to Hell, the rider's pleases me most.'

"They hesitated near the urn, their glances fixed, possessed by the same daemon. And all about, stretched along the rectangular lids, leaning on their left elbows, were the obese forms of the dead, thick stone lips half open in peace, holding in the right hand the crook, the fan, the tablets. But all the left hands were poised immutably on the cushions, strongly shaped, some enormous, others eaten away, mutilated, conveying to both a vague anguish, as if they had sensed the hands weighing on their hearts." (1)

A sudden break in Etruscan art

Though still ignorant of the precise makeup of Etruscan metaphysics, we are nonetheless aware of its sudden changes. Owing to the recent excavations carried out in Etruscan cities as far removed from one another as Marzabotto in the north and Caere in the south, we can see how radically the representation of the hereafter changed in the fifth century. (2)

Before this period, the tombs were actual funeral dwellings. The rooms where the bodies lay opened onto a corridor or were even arranged around an inner court. They were full of furniture and luxurious household items. The mural paintings depicted banquets, feasts, hunts, concerts and, most of all, war scenes where proud, slender Etruscan soldiers are seen striking down their enemies. The choice of bright colors and the harmonious bearings of the characters evoke a world of happiness and triumph. In these paintings Etruria appears confident, prosperous, victorious in

1. *Gabriele D'Annunzio,* La Città Morta, *as quoted in Hus,* The Etruscans, *trans. Jeanne Unger Duell (New York : Grove Press, 1961), pp. 7-8.*
2. *Marzabotto, ten miles from Bologna, is one of the rare sites in Great Etruria north of the Apennines that has yielded rich examples of Etruscan art.*

every way. As we have explained earlier, this was the era of Etruscan expansion.

Starting on the fifth century, everything changed radically. The colors became darker and less vivid. The bright reds and brilliant yellows gradually gave way to the colors of mourning, sadness, and death: deep purple, ochre red and midnight blue became the predominant colors of the funerary paintings. The somber spirit invading Etruscan pictorial art is even more evident in the representation of the characters. To be sure, the men, gods and demons continue holding banquets and feasts, but their postures lack freedom and spontaneity. Their gestures are strained, their faces anxious: Etruscan art is governed by hidden torment and anguish, which were to persist until the end of Etruscan civilization and its total disappearance.

The kingdom of the dead is no longer a pleasant group of tombs wonderfully arranged around an atrium, but rather a tenebrous world gaping into Hell. At the beginning of the fifth century, Etruria suffered its first setbacks: constant warfare against Rome and other Italic peoples, defeat on land and at sea by the Greeks of southern Italy, domestic struggles between Tarquinii and Vulci, Caere, and Clusium. Bit by bit the Etruscan confederation fell apart. The Etruscan empire was in the throes of death and her agony manifests itself in an ever more terrifying vision of Hell. (1)

1. We advise those interested in Etruscan art and its development to consult the very handsome book by Ranuccio Bianchi Bandinelli and Antonio Giuliano, Etruschi e Italici prima del dominio di Roma (Milan: Rizzoli, 1973). It has also been published in France by Gallimard (1973) in the famous series "L'Univers des formes" under the general editorship of André Malraux and André Parrot. Today

Faces twisted in pain and disfigured by horrifying grimaces

In this Etruscan Hell reigns a motley crew of demons and genii. Their number and names, as those of the gods, differ according to the various cities and periods. In the Sette Camini Tomb in Orvieto, Athrpa, a sort of Fury with a tormented face, may be seen enthroned in the midst of a funeral banquet. Elsewhere, in the Dell'Orco Tomb in Tarquinia, Lasa is seen presenting a scroll on which the deeds of the deceased are inscribed. In other sepulchers in Tarquinia and in Arezzo there are demons dressed in wolves' heads and three-headed monsters with four bird claws.

In the impressive necropolises at Volterra described by D'Annunzio, one finds Vanth, a disturbing winged female demon. Dressed in a long ochre-colored robe, she holds the Book of Fate in her hands and silently, impassively watches the agonies of the dying. Here Etruscan realism bursts forth with unusual violence: the faces of the dead are painted in colors evocative of wasted flesh and are twisted in pain, disfigured by horrifying grimaces. Another female demon, Culsu, is displayed, in certain tombs in Volsinii, brandishing torches and mercilessly hounding a procession of the dead. Many other menacing demons appear in the frescoes of Tuscan necropolises, devils with horns and

Bandinelli is editor in chief of the Enciclopedia dell'Arte antica, classica e orientale and Antonio Giuliano, a world-famous specialist of Etruscan painting, is director of the Archeological Institute at the University of Genoa.

cloven feet, armed with sticks and inflicting a thousand tortures on the dead.

Charun, the Etruscan demon of death

The absolute master of the Etruscan kingdom of the dead, however, and the sole demon displayed in almost all funeral paintings is Charun, to whom Franz de Ruyt has devoted a fascinating study. Despite its date *Charun, démon étrusque de la mort* (1934) remains an irreplaceable classic, a masterpiece that accomplishes the rare feat of integrating expert scholarship and clarity (in contrast to the many "scholarly" works that are nearly as difficult to read as Etruscan!)

"Charun first appears in the fifth century," writes Franz de Ruyt. "He even becomes omnipresent. He is the Mask of Death. It was as if death could and henceforth should be shown as being the future of us all, an idea which frightens us. We dare express and acknowledge this fear.

"Charun appeared in the shape of a man, a very ugly man, but a man all the same. The 'realism' with which he is painted is striking. His nose is huge and hooked, his ears long and pointed, his hair and beard unkempt, and his teeth gnash. This character has something horrible, bestial about him. In the paintings he is differentiated from men by his color; as a rule he is painted dark blue." (1)

1. *Franz de Ruyt,* Charun, démon étrusque de la mort *(Brussels: Editions de l'Insitut historique belge de Rome, 1934). This work was written under the direction of the great Belgian historian, Henri*

His protruding eyes are burning

Although the name of the demon Charun is derived from the famous Greek Charon, he is quite unlike the peaceable boatman of the Styx, the dutiful old man who, according to Greek legend, confined his activities to transporting the dead in his boat. The Etruscan Charun comes closer to the horrible demon described by the Etruscan-born Latin poet, Virgil:

> *terribili squalore Charon: cui plurima mento*
> *canities inculta iacet; stant lumina flamma;*
> *sordidus ex umeris nodo dependet amictus.*

> (Here was the hideous Charon,
> The keeper of this ford, revoltingly dirty,
> A matter straggle of white beard on his chin,
> His eyes glaring, a disgusting cloak
> Knotted and dangling from his shoulder.) (1)

On the very numerous sarcophagi where Charun is portrayed, the demon chastises, beats, and torments the dead that he has just welcomed into his eerie kingdom, and plagues them with the greatest variety of tortures. There is even a fresco found in Tarquinia where Charun is wresting a man from the embraces of his family and beating him to death with his mallet. On a

Pirenne, former president of the Managing Board of the Belgian Historical Institute of Rome, and Joseph Cuvelier, general archivist of the Kingdom of Belgium.
1. *Virgil, Aeneid, trans. Patric Dickinson (New York: Mentor, 1961), Bk. VI, p. 183.*

Chariot race: bas relief from a stone cippus. From Chiusi (province of Sienna) where there is a remarkable Etruscan necropolis. About 470 B.C. Palermo Museum. *(Rapho)*

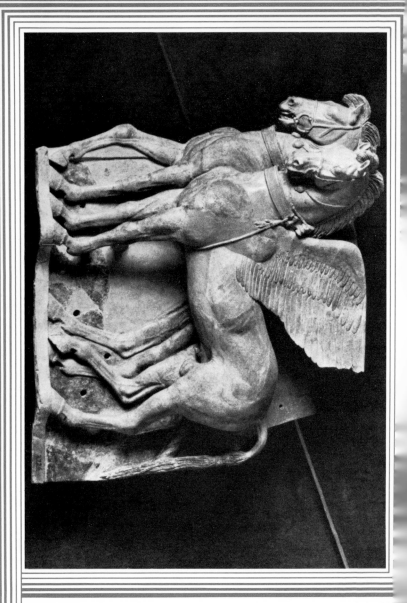

Terracotta group of winged horses (originally harnessed to a chariot). Archi[tectural] decoration from a temple at Tarquinia. About 300 B.C. Tarquinia M[useum]
(Giraudon)

stele in Bologna, Charun appears in the guise of a hirsute and terrifying giant on whose arm stand a horse and rider. On other steles—in Arezzo, Volsinii, and Tarquinia—Charun trails behind him a variety of animals including a sphinx, griffons, sea horses, sea monsters, and ravenous lions. Only one demon sheds any light and human warmth in Charun's dark and cruel realm, an anonymous male demon with regular features. "He is younger and more pleasant," notes Franz de Ruyt, "and he assists Charun in his duties, acting as a kind of foil to him."

From the Babylonian Nergal to the Etruscan Charun

Do the sufferings and torments inflicted by Charun last eternally in the hereafter? Do they imply that Etruscan theology assumed the immortality of the soul after death? This is what Franz de Ruyt believes. He compares Charun to the Assyro-Babylonian god Nergal, who has the same frightful countenance. He claims that Babylonian and Etruscan metaphysical visions have many points in common, and, in so doing, lends support to those who favor Anatolian origins for the Etruscans. Both peoples contemplated a life in the hereafter.

"Human nature," concludes the author, "does not change through the ages, nor do man's psychological responses, but their outward manifestations, determined by the contingencies of the hour and the evolution of ideas, do change. Charun, the Etruscan demon of death, is an aspect, *hic et nunc*, of human responses to that troubling mystery which inevitably pervades that equally strange and ungraspable phenomenon, life."

The Etruscan discipline

Although our knowledge of Etruscan metaphysics results only from comparison with other religions, we do possess a great many documents that give us a relatively precise and clear view of the practical aspects of Etruscan religion, aspects collectively grouped under the name "Etruscan discipline."

What exactly was this discipline? It was a body of rules covering the relationships between gods and man. Its starting point was the scrupulous inquiry into divine will by all possible means. Lightning, thunder, the entrails of sacrificed animals, the flight of birds, the orbit of the stars, the appearance of comets, rain, dreams and nightmares, hermaphrodites, two-headed children, premature births, trees, bees—everything served as an opportunity for the Etruscan magi, haruspices, and diviners to determine and forecast the future.

The "Etruscan discipline" was essentially divided into three parts: the art of interpreting lightning flashes, thunderbolts, and thunder; the art of reading the entrails of sacrificial victims; and third, the most subtle art of all, the appearance of prodigies whose profound meanings Etruscan diviners were supposed to decipher.

Divine signs sent to mortals

The art of interpreting thunder and lightning was set down in a few sacred Etruscan books, the books of lightning or *Libri fulgurales*. Like most Etruscan religious texts, these books have been lost; all that we have are a few references and anecdotes handed down to us by Seneca, Pliny, Cicero, Aulus-Gellius, and Nigidius Figulus.

Seneca explains that this art is based on the Etruscans' fundamental belief that signs were sent by the gods from heaven to inform mankind of their plans. It was therefore imperative that "those divine intentions" be interpreted.

"This is the difference," writes the Spanish-born Latin philosopher, "between us and the Etruscans, who have consummate skill in interpreting lightning: we think that because clouds collide lightning is emitted; they believe that clouds collide in order that lightning may be emitted. Since they attribute everything to divine agency they are of the opinion that things do not reveal the future because they have occurred, but that they occur because they are meant to reveal the future." (1)

Lightning that perforates, breaks, and burns

After having thus described the Etruscans' response to this celestial phenomenon, Seneca himself provides

1. *Seneca,* Natural Questions, *trans. Thomas H. Corcoran (Cambridge: Harvard University Press, 1971), Bk. II, 32 (p. 151).*

a classification of lightning which is based, he adds, on the indisputable expertise of Aulus Caecina, who came from a wealthy and educated Etruscan family in Volterra. He had been sent into exile by Caesar in Sicily and from there corresponded with Cicero, who believed him not only to be an excellent writer but also an expert in the art of divination. Cicero referred in a letter to "the truly marvelous teaching in the Etruscan discipline which you received from your father, whose merit equalled his birth." (1)

That was the authoritative source on which Seneca based his classification of lightning:

"Types of lightning are as follows: the type that bores, the type that scatters, and the type that burns. The one that bores is subtle and flaming. Because of the unmixed, pure thinness of its flame it finds escape through the narrowest openings. The type that scatters is a mass and has a great amount of condensed and stormy air mixed in it. Thus, the first type escapes by returning through that hole by which it entered. The second scatters its effects widely and breaks through whatever it strikes instead of perforating it.

"The third type, the one that burns, has a great deal of earthy element and is more fire than flame. And so it leaves great scars of fire which cling to the things struck. Actually, no lightning comes without fire, but we nonetheless properly call this type fiery because it imprints obvious traces of heat, and because it burns or blackens. It burns in three ways: it either scorches and damages with light marring, or burns up, or sets afire.

1. *Excerpt from a letter by Cicero to Caecina, quoted by Heurgon,* Daily Life of the Etruscans, *p. 234.*

All these cause burning but they differ in type and degree . . . .

"Now I pass on to the type of lightning which blackens the objects it strikes. This lightning either colors objects or discolors them. To each process I will grant the difference due to it. Something is discolored when its color is blemished, not changed. Something is colored when its appearance becomes other than it was, blue, for example, or black, or whitish." (1)

Bolts of lightning bursting out of the ground

Pliny, on the other hand, notes that according to "Etruscan writings" there are nine gods with the power to hurl lightning and twelve varieties of lightning, as three different types belong to Tinia-Jupiter. He also tells us of a strange Etruscan belief relating to bolts of lightning bursting out of the ground.

"Tuscany believes that some also burst out of the ground, which it calls 'low bolts,' and that these are rendered exceptionally direful and accursed by the season of winter, though all the bolts that they believe of earthly origin are not the ordinary ones and do not come from the stars but from the nearer and more disordered elements: a clear proof of this being that all those coming from the upper heaven deliver slanting blows, whereas these which they call earthly strike straight. And those that fall from the nearer elements are supposed to come out of the earth because they

1. *Seneca*, Natural Questions, *Bk. II, 39-40 (pp. 165-167).*

leave no traces as a result of their rebound, although that is the principle not of a downward blow but of a slanting one. Those who pursue these enquiries with more subtlety think that these bolts come from the planet Saturn, just as the inflammatory ones come from Mars, as, for instance, when Bolsena, the richest town in Tuscany, was entirely burnt up by a thunderbolt. Also the first ones that occur after a man sets up house for himself are called "family meteors," as foretelling his fortune for the whole of his life. However, people think that private meteors, except those that occur either at a man's first marriage or on his birthday, do not prophesy beyond ten years, nor public ones beyond the thirtieth year, except those occurring at the colonization of a town." (1)

It is unlawful to cremate a man struck by lightning

Pliny then explains the manner in which the Etruscan augurers differentiated favorable from unfavorable lightning. This art, whose past masters were the Etruscan diviners, persisted among the Romans long after the political disappearance of Etruria and its assimilation into the Roman Empire. Consequently, these diviners accompanied the Roman legions in their conquests, in order to search the skies for celestial omens and advise the generals to whom they were attached.

1. *Pliny,* Natural History, *trans. H. Rackham (1938; rpt. Cambridge: Harvard University Press, 1967), Bk. II, 53 (p. 275).*

"Flashes on the left," writes Pliny, "are considered lucky, because the sun rises on the left-hand side of the firmament; and their approach is not so visible as their return, whether after the blow a fire springs from it or the breath returns when its work is done or its fire used up.

"In making these observations the Tuscans divided the heavens into sixteen parts: the first quarter is from the North, to the equinoctial sunrise (East), the second to the South, the third to the equinoctial sunset (West), and the fourth occupies the remaining space extending from West to North; these quarters they subdivided into four parts each, of which they called the eight starting from the East the left-hand regions and the eight opposite ones the right-hand. Of these the most formidable are those lying between West and North. Hence the line of approach and the line of retirement of thunderbolts are of very great importance. It is best for them to return to parts in the region of sunrise. Accordingly it will be a portent of supreme happiness when they come from the first part of the sky and retire to the same part—a sign that history records to have been vouchsafed to the dictator Sulla: but all the others are less fortunate or actually direful, in accordance with the division of the actual firmament where they occur. Some people think it wrong to give or to listen to reports of thunderbolts, except when given to a guest or a parent.

"The great folly of paying attention to these occurrences was discovered when the Temple of Juno at Rome was struck by lightning in the consulship of Scaurus, who was afterwards head of the State.

"Lightning unaccompanied by thunder occurs more often by night than in the daytime. Man is the one creature not always killed when struck—all others are killed on the spot; nature doubtless bestows this honor on man because so many animals surpass him in strength. All things (when struck) fall in the opposite direction to the flash. A man does not die unless the force of the blow turns him right around. Men struck from above collapse. A man struck while awake is found with his eyes shut; while asleep with them open. It is not lawful to cremate a man who loses his life in this manner; religious tradition prescribes burial. No living creature can be burnt by lightning without being killed. The temperature of the wound of those struck is lower than that of the rest of the body." (1)

An exceptionally informative calendar

There is, in this field of celestial phenomena which intensely preoccupied the Etruscans, a very important document relating to thunders which we referred to earlier in this book: the brontoscopic calendar of Nigidius Figulus. This Latin philosopher, a contemporary of Cicero and a man well versed in Orphic mysticism, maintains that he had obtained his calendar "from an indisputable Etruscan source."

Here is how this calendar is presented. The author follows the sequence of months beginning June 1; they are all 30 days in length, even February, and there is no

1. *Pliny, Bk. II, 55 (p. 279).*

intercalated month. The meaning of thunder is indicated for each day of the month, forecasting a happy event relating either to agriculture or to social or public life. This brontoscopic calendar thus not only tells us about the Etruscans' religious superstitions but also reveals much about their way of life. The importance accorded to harvesting, animals, fruits and agricultural activities in general expresses how closely this nation of peasants was tied to its land.

Thanks to this calendar, we know that the Etruscans grew wheat and barley, raised sheep and cattle, ate saltwater and freshwater fish, feared wild animals, grasshoppers and floods, and welcomed rain because frequent droughts forced them to import their food supply one year out of two.

Besides this agricultural information, the brontoscopic calendar provides political information about Etruscan cities. We discover thereby that Etruria had a queen-city (Tarquinia) and several subject-cities. In the queen-city, power seems to have been in the hands of a powerful ruling minority. There was constant conflict between the powerful and the people. A king is referred to constantly, by turns described as "master of all matters," "tyrant," or "magnificent lord."

The calendar emphasizes above all the theme of civil strife. Strange as it may seem, "dissension" is the most frequently encountered word in the calendar (43 times). The threat of tyranny was born of this strife. There are constant appeals for peace among the inhabitants of the city. At the head of the government was a Senate, which apparently did not succeed in establishing peace and harmony between the rulers and the often rebellious and sometimes victorious masses. Therefore, Etruscan social equilibrium was quite fragile, threatened as it was by civil uprisings, assassinations, and conspiracies. (1)

A vivid, fascinating portrait of Etruscan life

According to the French translation of the brontoscopic calendar by Louis Legrand, the multiple meanings of thunder provided day by day for the entire month of June are as indicated below. As Legrand puts it so well, this will help us "to mix with the average Etruscan, to enter into intimate contact with his daily life, to discover both his religious and practical preoccupations, to speculate on his fears, his hopes, in short, to see him live. No other text gives us such a vivid, fascinating and authentic picture of daily life as it unfolded in the land of Etruria."

Therefore, here is this document; as the first phrase "If it thunders" is systematically repeated at the beginning of each day, it has been eliminated, except for the first day of the month of June.

«June 1—If it thunders, there will be abundant

1. *We have gathered our information of the brontoscopic calendar from two sources: the highly scholarly and, unfortunately for the layman, almost unreadable article by André Piganiol published 1973 in the review* Scripta varia *(vol. 132), and the admirably clear thesis devoted to "Publius Nigidius Figulus, philosophe néo-pythagoricien orphique" by Louis Legrand in 1930. This unpublished dissertation may be found in the Library of the Sorbonne under the reference HF uf 112 to 428. This thesis is one of the most detailed studies of Etruscan divination ever done, and is still cited even in the most recent works on the subject.*

harvests, except for barley; man will be afflicted by dangerous illness.

June 2—Giving birth will be less painful for mothers; cattle will die; fish will be plentiful.

June 3—There will be very dry heat waves; also, not only dry fruit but also soft fruit will be completely scorched by the drought.

June 4—The weather will be so humid and rainy that the crops will rot and be lost.

June 5—Harm will come to the countryside. Those who govern cities and small towns will have problems.

June 6—A destructive insect will hatch amid the already ripe crop.

June 7—Sickness will occur; however, very few will die. Dry fruits will do well, the others will dry out.

June 8—There will be plenty of rain and the wheat will die.

June 9—Flocks will be killed by attacking wolves.

June 10—There will be many deaths but the harvests will be plentiful.

June 11—Mild heat spells; the republic will be prosperous.

June 12—Same as preceding day.

June 13—A very powerful man will be threatened with ruin.

June 14—The air will be hot; nevertheless there will be a very good harvest and fish will also be plentiful in the rivers. However, bodies will be sickly.

June 15—Winged creatures will be highly indisposed by the summer; the fish will die.

June 16—Both a drop in the harvest and a war are forecast; a very wealthy man will disappear.

June 17—There will be prosperity; rats, moles, and grasshoppers will die; however, the year will bring both wealth and murder to the Roman people.

June 18—A disastrous shortage of fruit is expected.

June 19—Animals harmful to fruits will die.

June 20—Menace of strife among the Romans.

June 21—A wine shortage is forecast but there will be plenty of other products and fish.

June 22—The heat will be disastrous.

June 23—Joy, the end of evil, recovery from sickness are announced.

June 24—An abundance of goods is promised.

June 25—There will be innumerable wars and misfortunes.

June 26—Winter will ruin the harvests.

June 27—The leaders of the republic will be threatened by the army.

June 28—The harvests will be plentiful.

June 29—City affairs will improve.

June 30—There will soon be many deaths."

A single bolt of lightning killed a bull and five cows

At the end of the thesis from which this brontoscopic almanac was taken, Louis Legrand stresses its secret, esoteric nature. As with all Etruscan sacred books, it was reserved exclusively for the haruspices entrusted with deciphering the will of the gods by carefully observing and wisely interpreting signs from the sky: thunderclaps, thunderbolts, lightning flashes, or rain. The numerous testimonies left to us by the Roman chroniclers bear witness to the great importance of divination both in Tuscan society and later in Roman society, which fervently adopted the "Etruscan discipline" in its entirety.

"In a city which was at the highest pitch of excitement about the new war," writes Livy, "during a storm at night the *columna rostrata* [a column adorned with the beaks of captured ships], which had been set up on the Capitoline in the first Punic war in honor of the victory of the consul Marcus Aemilius, whose colleague was Servius Fulvius, was completely destroyed by lightning. This event was regarded as a prodigy and was referred to the Senate; the Fathers ordered that the matter should be referred to the haruspices and, moreover, that the decemvirs [10-member ruling bodies] should consult the Books. The decemvirs reported back that the city should be purified, that a period of supplication and prayer should be held, and that sacrifices of full-grown victims should be offered both on the Capitoline at Rome and in Campania at the promontory of Minerva; further, that at the earliest possible moment games for ten days should be celebrated in honor of Jupiter Optimus Maximus. All these directions were scrupulously obeyed. The haruspices pronounced that this omen would turn out for the best, and that an extension of frontiers and the destruction of the enemy were foretold, because those beaks which the storm had overthrown had been spoils taken from the enemy. Other occurrences also increased their concern to appease the gods: news had been brought that at Saturnia there were showers of blood in the town on three successive days; that at Calatia an ass with three feet was born and a bull with five cows was killed by a single bolt of lightning; that at Auximum a shower of earth had fallen. By reason of these prodigies also sacrifices were offered and a day of prayer and a festival were celebrated."(1)

"When soothsayers from all Etruria had gathered there"

Nor did Cicero fail to consult the Etruscan haruspices when the Republic was in danger. He devoted long, laudatory passages to them. In his *Third Oration Against Catiline,* in which the Roman orator gives an account of Catiline's conspiracy, Cicero relates an episode which took place in 61 B.C. During that year, numerous celestial phenomena—lightning, earthquakes, meteors—threw the Roman people into a state of fear and panic:

"Not to mention the torches and fiery glow in the western sky at night, the crash of thunderbolts, the succession of earth tremors, and other phenomena manifested so often in such quantity in my consulship that it looked as if the immortal gods were predicting the events now taking place; yet, what I do want to say must neither be omitted nor unintentionally over-

1. Livy, *trans. Evan T. Sage and Alfred C. Schlesinger (1938; rpt. Cambridge: Harvard University Press, 1964), Bk. XLII, 20 (pp. 347-349). Unless otherwise specified, quotations of Livy's work in this chapter are from the 14-volume Loeb Classical Library edition published jointly by William Heinemann Ltd., in London, and Harvard University Press, in Cambridge, Massachussets, under the general editorship of E. T. Paige.*

looked. Surely you remember how, in the consulship of
Cotta and Torquatus, many things in the Capitol were
struck by lightning: the statues of the gods were
toppled, statues of ancient heroes overturned, the
bronze tablets of the law liquefield; and even our
founder Romulus was wounded—as you recall the
wound shows in the scar on the golden statue on the
Capitoline of the infant drinking at the wolf's teats.
At that time, when soothsayers from all Etruria had
gathered there, they declared that massacre, conflagra-
tion, the extinction of law and order, civil war, revolt,
the fall of the entire city and its imperial authority, were
drawing near, unless the immortal gods were placated
in every way possible, so that their intercession might
deflect what destiny had decreed.

"Because of their pronouncements, a 10-day festival period was proclaimed, and nothing was overlooked that might serve to conciliate the gods. The
soothsayers also ordered that a large statue of Jove be
made and set up in a high place facing east, in the
opposite direction from the previous statue, which you
can see here today, and that by looking out over the
sunrise and the Forum and the Senate house, it would
bring to light the secret plans being formed to under-
mine the security of the city and its imperial authority,
and would make them visible to the Senate and the
Roman people."(1)

1. *Cicero,* Nine Orations, *trans. Palmer Bovie (New York: Mentor,
1967), p. 143.*

Two white cows and twenty-seven virgins

In another anecdote, Livy shows how closely the instructions prescribed by the Etruscan augurers were followed, down to the most minute detail. The slightest omission, so thought the Romans, could lead to serious accidents and disturb the city's social and political equilibrium. This balance had to be preserved at all costs, precisely by means of the techniques of the Etruscan magi.

"The temple of Juno the Queen on the Aventine," writes Livy, "was struck by lightning. That this portent concerned the matrons was opinion of the soothsayers, and that the goddess must be appeased by a gift; whereupon the matrons domiciled in the city of Rome or within ten miles of it were summoned by an edict of the curule aediles to the Capitol. And from their own number they themselves chose twenty-five, to whom they should bring a contribution from their dowries. Out of that a gold basin was made as a gift and carried to the Aventine, and the matrons after due purification offered sacrifice.

"At once a day was appointed by the decemvirs for another sacrifice to the same goddess; and the order of procedure was as follows: from the Temple of Apollo two white cows were led through the Porta Carmentalis into the city; behind them were carried two statues of Juno the Queen in cypress wood. Then the seven and twenty maidens in long robes marched, singing their hymn in honor of Juno the Queen, a song which to the untrained minds of that time may have deserved praise, but now, if repeated, would be repellent and uncouth.

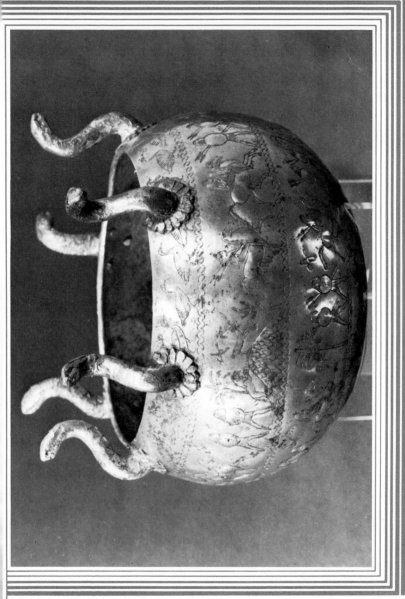

Large silver gilt vase decorated with hunting scenes and six snake protomes. From the Bernardini Tomb, Praeneste. Middle of the seventh century B.C. Pigorini Museum, Rome. *(Giraudon)*

Fragment of a fresco in the Tomb of the Augurs at Tarquinia. Two *agono*(umpires) surrounded by various other figures. About 530 B.C. *(Rapho-L*

Behind the company of maidens followed the decemvirs wearing laurel garlands and purple-bordered
togas. From the gate they proceeded along the Vicus
Iugarius into the Forum. In the Forum the procession
halted, and passing a rope from hand to hand the
maidens advanced, accompanying the sound of their
voices by beating time with their feet . . . ." (1)

Treacherous haruspices sentenced to death

The Roman chronicles are filled with these types of
stories and anecdotes, which emphasize the indispensable role played in the city by the Etruscan magi,
diviners, and haruspices. As long as the Etruscan magi
abided by the "true principles" of divination they were
praised, feasted, and showered with gifts and prestige,
but as soon as they resorted to fraud and misused their
knowledge they were mercilessly punished, as indicated in the report of this incident by Aulus-Gellius in
his *Attic Nights*:

"The statue of that bravest of men, Horatius Cocles,
which stood in the Comitium at Rome, was struck by
lightning. To make expiatory offerings because of that
thunderbolt, diviners were summoned from Etruria.
These, through personal and national hatred of the
Romans, had made up their minds to give false directions for the performance of that rite. They accordingly
gave the misleading advice that the statue in question
should be moved to a lower position, on which the sun

1. Livy, *trans. Frank Gardner Moore (Cambridge: Harvard University
Press, 1963), Bk. XXVII, 37 (pp. 359-361).*

never shone, being cut off by the high buildings which surrounded the place on every side. When they had induced the Romans to take that course, they were betrayed and brought to trial before the people, and having confessed their duplicity, were put to death. And it became evident, in exact accord with what were later found to be proper directions, that the statue ought to be taken to an elevated place and set up in a more commanding position in the area of Vulcan; and after that was done, the matter turned out happily and successfully for the Romans. At that time, then, because the evil counsel of the Etruscan diviners had been detected and punished, this clever line is said to have been composed, and chanted by the boys all over the city: 'Bad counsel to the giver is most ruinous.'

"This story about the diviners and that verse is found in the *Annales Maximi,* in the eleventh book of *Things Worth Remembering.* But the verse appears to be a translation of the Greek poet Hesiod's familiar verse: 'And evil counsel most evil is / To him who gives it.''(1)

A very valuable source: the Piacenza liver

Next to the interpretation of lightning, thunder, and other celestial phenomena, haruspicy, or examination of the viscera of sacrificed victims, constituted the second branch of the Etruscan discipline. Among the viscera, the liver holds a special place. The basic

1. The Attic Nights of Aulus Gellius, *trans. John C. Rolfe (1927; rpt. Cambridge: Harvard University Press, 1961), Bk. IV, 5 (pp. 327-329).*

principle of Etruscan haruspicy may be stated as follows: every sacred object reproduces the divine image of the universe. In the sacrificed animal, the liver, which according to the Etruscans is the very seat of life, is to some extent a mirror of the state of the world at the time the victim was slaughtered. This is why favorable or unfavorable omens, and generally all the inventions of the gods, may be discerned in it. Provided he is skillful and inspired, a haruspex may decipher the gods' most subtle, most recondite intentions by careful inspection of the liver.(1)

A very valuable source on this Etruscan haruspicy is available: it is the famous Piacenza liver, mentioned earlier. Georges Dumézil has devoted a remarkable study to it which is, however, too complex to be summarized here. It is enough to say that in his view the Piacenza liver symbolizes the well-known Indo-European opposition of round and square.(2)

Arruns the diviner turned pale and snatched up the entrails

The French Etruscologist Jacques Heurgon believes that the Piacenza liver, whose inscriptions are far from completely deciphered and properly interpreted, was produced in Cortona, a city where it seems Etruscan religion had survived longer than anywhere else. ''The

1. *This is a short summary of Albert Grenier's important article, "L'orientation du foie de Plaisance,"* published in the Revue des études latines *in 1946.*
2. *Georges Dumézil,* Archaic Roman Religion.

liver probably fell from the baggage of a traveling
haruspex near the crossroads at Piancenza, maybe one
of those haruspices attached to a general in the field or
a province governor," he speculates, adding that "the
careless haruspex" might well have been the famous
Spurinna, Caesar's augurer, who is mentioned by the
Roman historian Suetonius!

As we have stated, the liver has privileged status in
Etruscan haruspicy. This does not mean, however, that
other parts of the viscera, such as the intestines, the
heart or the lungs, are overlooked. Each detail is important, as certified by this passage from Lucan's *The
Civil War* (better known as *The Pharsalia*), where we
witness a sacrifice conducted by the Etruscan diviner
Arruns. This is a valuable document which manages to
restore for us the intensity that pervaded the magic
divinatory practices of the Etruscans. Lucan writes:

"When he [Arruns] began to pour wine and to
sprinkle meal with slanting knife, the victim struggled
long against the unacceptable sacrifice; but when the
high-girt attendants thrust down its formidable horns,
it sank to the ground and offered its helpless neck to the
blow. No red blood spouted forth from the gaping
wound, but a slimy liquid, strange and dreadful, came
out instead. Appalled by the funereal rite, Arruns turned
pale and snatched up the entrails, to seek there the
anger of the gods. Their very color alarmed him: the
sickly spots, colored with concealed gore, and check-
ered all over with dark patches and bloodspots. He saw
the liver flabby with corruption and with ominous
streaks in its hostile half. The extremity of the panting
lung was invisible, and a thin membrane divided the

vital organs. The heart was flattened, the entrails exuded corrupted blood through gaping cracks, and the caul revealed its hiding-place. And lo! he saw a horror which never yet was seen in a victim's entrails without mischief following: a great second lobe was growing upon the lobe of the liver; one half drooped, sickly and flabby, while the other throbbed fast and drove the veins with rapid beat. When thus he had grasped the prediction of great disaster, he cried aloud: 'Scarce may I reveal to men's ears all the ills that the gods are preparing. Not with mightiest Jupiter has this my sacrifice found favor; but the infernal gods have entered into the body of the slaughtered bull. What we fear is unspeakable; but the sequel will be worse than our fears. May the gods give a favorable turn to what we have witnessed! May the entrails prove false, and may the lore of our founder Tages turn out to be mere imposture!' Thus the Toscan told the future, veiling it in obscurity and hiding it which much ambiguity."(1)

The viscera do not palpitate as usual

Seneca describes in his drama *Oedipus* the methods used by the haruspices to learn the will of the gods. Tiresias and his daughter Manto perform a sacrifice in the presence of Oedipus and seem terrified by the anomalies observed in the viscera. As in

1. *Lucan,* The Civil War, *trans. J. D. Duff (Cambridge: Harvard University Press, 1928), Bk. I, 609-638 (p. 47).*

Etruscan haruspicy, every anomaly signifies a distur-
bance in the natural order of things and therefore
heralds an evil omen.

"*Manto* : Father, what is this? The vibration of the
entrails is not faint, as is usually the case; they are
shaking both my hands, and fresh blood is spurting
from the veins. The heart is diseased and shrunken and
deeply hidden; its veins are livid. The rotten liver is
missing a great part of its fiber, and oozing black gall.
Look—this is always a bad sign for monarchy—two
heads rise with equal swelling, and each severed head
is covered with a thin membrane; there is no hiding of
secrets. The hostile side is raised and rugged, with
seven taut veins, but an oblique line intercepts them
and prevents their turning back."(1)

Sometimes, the examination of viscera can yield
ambiguous results. Although, in the case cited by
Seneca, the seven veins located on the "hostile side"
leave not the slightest doubt as to the wrath of the gods,
the following anecdote of Livy's shows how the
haruspex must act with subtlety and discrimination
upon "reading" divine signs, especially if they are
ambiguous.

"The Roman consuls," relates Livy, "before leading
their troops into battle offered sacrifices. It is said that
the soothsayer pointed out to Decius that the head of
the liver was wounded on the friendly side; but that the
victim was in all other respects acceptable to the gods,
and that the sacrifice of Manlius had been greatly

1. *Seneca,* Oedipus, *trans. Moses Hadas, in* Roman Drama *(Indianapolis: Bobbs-Merrill, 1965), Act II, scene 2 (p. 410).*

successful. 'It is well enough,' said Decius, 'if my colleague has received favorable tokens.'"(1)

The interpretation is ambiguous: a bad omen in a favorable region. The haruspex therefore predicted to Decius that he would gain victory but that he would die during the battle. "This is what happened," concludes Livy.

Prodigies—warnings from the gods to men

Etruscan magi and haruspices were not only supposed to grasp the hidden meaning of viscera or celestial phenomena; they also had to interpret prodigies. This is the third branch of the Etruscan discipline. In Etruscan religious life, a prodigy possesses inherent value to the same degree as thunder, lightning, or the quivering of entrails. The appearance of a prodigy indeed disturbs the natural order of things, which is so important to Etruscan religious sensibility. It brutally disrupts the normal course of life for both individuals and communities, and therefore constitutes a warning from the gods to mortals. A prodigy may be either a good or a bad omen.

"A prodigy," notes Raymond Bloch, "is always the sacred bursting forth within the secular, and bears witness to various changes in the relationship between gods and men: the latter may infer information which is important to their own lives. The prodigy is a privileged

1. Livy, *trans. B. O. Foster (1926; rpt. Cambridge: Harvard University Press, 1963), Bk. VIII, 9 (p. 35).*

sign offered for human scrutiny and is therefore an integral part of the divinatory process, the preeminent religious activity of the Etruscans about which so many different literary, epigraphical, and archeological documents have informed us."(1)

The weight of the mysterious forces of destiny

Examining one after another the particular attitude of the Greeks, Etruscans, and Romans toward prodigies, Raymond Bloch notes that the art of interpreting them was widespread, albeit to varying degrees, among the peoples of antiquity. It was a highly complex art, consisting in deriving from supernatural phenomena precise indications concerning the past, present and future.

The author emphasizes how the essentially rationalist Greeks conceded little importance to those manifestations that were foreign to the natural order of things. "On the other hand," he adds, "the Etruscans, who constantly felt burdened by the weight of the mysterious forces of destiny, devoted their full attention and their ritualistic sciences to it. As for the Romans, they were sufficiently superstitious to regularly observe prodigies around them, but were also pragmatic enough to firmly establish a ritual method of inquiry, which dealt with their existence so as to

1. *Raymond Bloch,* Les Prodiges dans l'Antiquité classique *(Paris: Presses universitaires de France, 1963). This work, published in the series "Mythes et religions" under the direction of Georges Dumézil, examines the science of prodigies among the Greeks, the Etruscans, and the Romans, and demonstrates how indebted the Romans were to the Etruscans in this field.*

emphasize their optimistic character and minimize their threatening aspect. The attitude of the people of anti-quity toward prodigies has probably best defined the characteristics of their religion and genius."

"Rome will never take Veii until the Alban lake is drained"

Almost nothing remains of the sacred Etruscan tests describing the art of "decoding" the prodigies—con-stituting the "coded language" used by the immortal gods to communicate with man. All these texts have been lost as part of the overall disappearance of Etruscan literature. Nevertheless, in translations and references by Greek and Latin authors, a few scattered fragments—very short ones, to be sure—have sur-vived to inform us in quite a precise fashion about the practices of the Tuscan magi and the principles that they used to decipher the divine will by means of prodigies, before conjuration with the appropriate ex-piatory ceremonies capable of appeasing the wrath of the gods. Here we find the fundamental trait of Etruscan religiosity: appeasing celestial anger by expiatory rites meant nothing other than reestablishing the natural order disrupted by the appearance of a prodigy.(1)

One of the most frequently cited examples used to illustrate the substantial role played by prodigies

1. *This is merely a very brief summary of J. Bayet's fascinating article published in the* Annuaire de l'Institut de philologie et d'histoire orientales et slaves *(Brussels: Mélanges Franz Cumont, 1936). This highly scholarly work, despite its age, is still a basic source.*

among Etruscans has to do with the lake of Alba. The story, related at length by Livy, takes place during the siege by Roman troops of the Etruscan city, Veii, in the beginning of the fourth century B.C. The siege had been going on for many months and the Roman besiegers had begun to lose heart when a prodigy occurred, as the Roman historian relates:

"The lake in the Alban Wood, without any unusual rainfall or other natural cause, rose much above its normal height. The thing was a prodigy, and a mission was dispatched to the Delphic oracle to inquire what the gods might mean by it. Meanwhile, however, an interpreter of the Fates presented himself nearer home in the person of an old man of Veii, who, while Roman and Etruscan soldiers were exchanging chaff as they faced each other on their respective guard-posts, suddenly burst out into prophecy and declared that Rome would never take Veii until the water in the Alban lake was drained off.

"An Etruscan diviner burst out into prophecy"

"At first the soldiers merely laughed, taking what the old fellow said as a meaningless gibe; but after a minute or two they began to talk it over, and finally one of them asked a man belonging to the town (the war had gone on so long that Romans and their enemies frequently talked to each other) to identify the old fellow who had made the mysterious remark about the Alban lake. The answer was that he was a soothsayer. Now the Roman sentry who had asked the question was of a superstitious turn of mind, so pretending a wish to consult the soothsayer, should he be able to spare the time, about some private puzzle of his own, he got him to come out and talk to him. Neither was armed, and they had walked off together some distance in apparently perfect mutual confidence, when the sentry, who was young and strong, suddenly seized his aged companion and carried him bodily to the Roman lines. The Etruscans who saw the act—indeed, it was obvious to everyone—raised a tremendous outcry but could do nothing to stop it.

"The soothsayer was taken to headquarters and then sent on to the Senate in Rome, where he was asked to explain what he had meant. In reply he said that the gods must indeed have been angry with Veii on the day when they put it into his mind to reveal the doom which was destined to fall upon his country, and for that reason what he had then been inspired to speak he could not now retract as if it had never been spoken ; for it might well be that it was as great a sin to conceal what the gods wished to be known as to speak what should remain concealed. He went on to say that it was known to Etruscan lore and written in the books of fate that, if the Romans drained the water from the Alban lake after it had risen high, they would be granted victory over Veii ; till then, the gods of Veii would never desert her city walls. He then began to explain in detail the proper method of drawing off the water . . . .

"When the mission arrived back from Delphi, the oracle they brought with them agreed with the prophecy of the old soothsayer who had been carried off from Veii. 'Let not, O Roman' (it ran) 'the Alban water be contained within its lake; let it not flow with its own stream to the sea. Thou shalt draw it out and water thy fields with it; thou shalt disperse it in rivulets and put out its power. Then mayst thou take courage and thrust against the enemy's walls, remembering that over the city, which for so long thou hast besieged, victory has been granted thee by the Fates which are now revealed. When the war is done and thou hast conquered, bring to my temple a rich gift and restore and celebrate in the fashion of thy fathers the sacred rites thou hast neglected.' ''(1)

The Romans followed the Etruscan diviner's prescriptions to the letter. They dug several canals. Within a few days, the Lake of Alba was drained and her waters flooded all the surrounding countryside. A short while later, the siege was lifted and Veii fell into the hands of the Romans in 396 B.C.

Subterranean rumbling, a formidable, incomprehensible phenomenon

Another text, this one by Cicero, gives us the form and content of a reply to the Senate by the Etruscan haruspices in 56 B.C. That year a violent subterranean rumbling had been heard in the *ager latiniensis* in Rome and had spread confusion throughout the population of the city.

At first, according to Cicero at least, the diviners limited themselves to carefully observing the prodigy

1. *Livy,* The Early History of Rome*, Bk. V, 15 (p. 342).*

they had been called to interpret: "Whereas, in the *ager latiniensis,* a rattling was heard accompanied by a tremor..." This was the first phase of the operation; a simple report of the phenomenon. Secondly, after many sophisticated magical operations, the haruspices managed to discover the names of the gods who had employed this rumbling to communicate their displeasure: this is how the complex interpretation of the prodigy began. This exegetic process was the focal point of the augural consultation since it gave the anxious city an explanation of the formidable and incomprehensible phenomenon. "The complaints," the Etruscan haruspices intoned on that occasion, no doubt in an appropriately sepulchral voice, "come from Jupiter, Saturn, Neptune, and Tellus...."

Terrible threats endanger the city

Why were these gods angry? In the third phase of this consultation, the diviners answered the question the Roman Senate had asked. The Etruscan magi gave a remarkably detailed and varied list of causes that might have provoked the gods' wrath. "The games have been carelessly celebrated and have been defiled. Holy and religious places have been desecrated for secular use. Orators have been executed, in contempt of laws both human and divine. Promises and oaths have been forgotten. Ancient and secret sacrifices have been performed too carelessly and have been defiled."

This terrifying report threw the Senate into panic: so many crimes, so many sacrileges and profanations

could not go unpunished, and the gods would surely
chastise a city guilty of these grave violations of divine
law! The senators then questioned the Etruscan
diviners: what perils threatened the citizens of Rome?
Once again—in this fourth phase of the operation—the
diagnosis was dreadful. In no way did the haruspices
attempt to humor the powerful senators of Rome. They
were the mouthpieces of the will of the gods and were
duty bound to expose the terrible dangers that threatened Rome. "Because of discord and dissent among
the *optimates* [the best men]," they therefore said, "it
is to be feared that murder and danger are being pre-
pared against fathers and leaders, that they will be deprived of help, as a result of which the provinces will
become subject to a single authority, the army will be
driven away, and a final collapse will occur. It is also to
be feared that wrongs will be committed against the
public welfare through secret dealings, that disrepu-
table men who have been thrown out of office will
attain powerful positions and finally that the form of
government will be changed."

The Etruscan haruspices, defenders of
the established order

Cicero's text, unfortunately, does not relate the fifth
and final phase of this operation, that is, the expiatory
rites which the Etruscan haruspices no doubt prescribed to the Roman senators in order to eliminate
such perils.

In spite of this omission, the text we have just

quoted is extremely revealing. It sheds light on the skill of the Etruscan magi in studying prodigies and gives quite a clear notion of the procedures followed in these haruspical ceremonies, which persisted almost until the collapse of the Roman Empire. It also reveals—and, in our opinion, herein lies the value of this text—a highly important political and social function of Etruscan diviners in Roman society. In reality, owing to its haruspices, diviners, magi, and priests, conquered Etruria survived to impose its rites, beliefs, and superstitions upon Rome. As Henry Harrel-Courtès has so aptly phrased it, "It is the victory of the vanquished."

Exactly what role did this Etruscan clergy play? Raymond Bloch explains that essentially they had a stabilizing role that consisted in transposing the wise precepts of religion into the sphere of politics. Social ills and rebellions disrupt a society's equilibrium to the same degree as the appearance of a prodigy disturbs the natural harmony of the universe. And one must struggle at all costs against these ills and attacks on human and divine order.

"The haruspices' fundamentally aristocratic attitude," writes Raymons Bloch, "is manifest in their announcement of the dangers that threaten the state and senatorial class. They repeat again and again their warnings against all attempts to overthrow the established order .... Throughout their responses one finds an apparent conservative bias which quite accurately reflects their regular stance .... The haruspices are supporters of the established order, the champions of the oligarchic class .... Their attitude was constant for the incredible duration of their religious practice, from the beginnings of Etruria to the end of the Roman Empire.''(1)

Preserve the college of the haruspices at all costs

Far from vanishing upon the political collapse of Etruria, therefore, the Etruscan discipline actually survived and prospered throughout Roman history. In his aforementioned treatise, *De Divinatione,* Cicero tells of a Senate resolution dating from the second century, inviting each of the twelve Etruscan city-states to send six young people of noble lineage to the Roman state to engage in religious studies and thus to perpetuate the Etruscan discipline. This Senate resolution prompted the Etruscan city-states to preserve their religious traditions so that, in the words of Cicero, ''such a great art might not be lost forever.''

In addition to the Senate resolution reported by Cicero, another document bears testimony to Rome's keen interest in Etruscan haruspicy; this document consists of a speech given before the Senate by the Emperor Claudius in A.D. 47. An ardent enthusiast of Etruria's glorious history—to which, as we noted, he devoted 20 volumes, now lost—the Emperor Claudius revealed to the senators his desire to stave off the invasion of foreign superstitions that were threatening to supplant ''Etruria's oldest science'' by Judaism or by Egyptian rites. The Emperor therefore urged the senators to protect the college of the haruspices, made

1. *Raymond Block,* Prodiges de l'Antiquité classique.

up of forty Etruscan diviners from the various Etruscan cities.

The text of this speech, as handed down by Tacitus, is as follows:

"Claudius then proposed to the Senate the establishment of a Board of Soothsayers. 'This oldest Italian art,' he said, 'ought not to die out through neglect. The advice of soothsayers, consulted in time of disaster, has often caused the revival and more correct subsequent observance of religious ceremonies. Moreover leading Etruscans, on their own initiative—or the Roman Senate's—have kept up the art and handed it down from father to son. Now, however, public indifference to praiseworthy accomplishments has caused its neglect; and the advance of foreign superstitions has contributed to this. At present all is well. But gratitude for divine favor must be shown by ensuring that rites observed in bad times are not forgotten in prosperity.' So the Senate decreed that the priests should consider which institutions of the soothsayers required upkeep or support."(1)

The common people turned toward licentiousness

In his *Histoire de la Divination,* A. Bouché-Leclercq notes that Emperor Claudius' admonishment about

1. Tacitus on Imperial Rome, *trans. Michael Grant, Bk. XI, 15 (p. 232). This text was quoted by A. Bouché-Leclercq in his admirable* Histoire de la divination *(Paris, 1879-1882), 4 vols. It has recently been republished in Brussels (1963) by Editions Culture et Civilisations. Volume IV is devoted entirely to Etruscan religion.*

"foreign superstitions" was directed not only against Egyptian rites and Judaism but especially against the Greek cult of Dionysius.

The Viennese archeologist Paul Frischauer has devoted a lengthy study precisely to the introduction of these highly licentious cults in Rome and Etruria during the first century B.C. It was a tumultuous period, replete with such modern controversies as divorce, the equality of men and women, and sexual freedom! Such debates were apparently little different from those we now read about in our daily papers:

"The divorce laws," writes Frischauer, "no longer worked exclusively in favor of the husband. Fewer and fewer indissoluble marriages were formed.... Social conventions were strictly adhered to in the patrician palaces decorated with refined Greek art, especially since the common people shamelessly turned toward unbridled licentiousness. The aristocrats wanted to stand apart, at least outwardly, from the degenerate masses. What took place behind four walls only leaked out slowly through the gossip of rejected lovers revenging themselves by writing. But the excesses of the men and women among the masses ... were a favorite subject of senatorial debates." (1)

1. *Paul Frischauer,* Archéologie de la sexualité *(Stock, 1969). The last and longest part of this work deals with sexuality among the Etruscans and is based for the most part on the funeral paintings discovered in Etruscan necropolises.*

No secret festivities may be held

To put a stop to this sexual profligacy and these orgies, which by the principles of the Etruscan discipline were held to be veritable outrages against the natural order, the Senate passed many laws threatening the degenerate with the direst of punishments.

"It is illegal for a Roman citizen to mingle with the followers of Bacchus. No man is allowed to become their priest. Men and women are forbidden to lead them, to share common funds or employees, or to hire either man or woman as an employee.... No secret festivities may be held which involve more than five persons. Among these no more than two men and three women are allowed.... The Bacchanalia shall be abolished ten days after the reading of this law."(1)

"A dabbler in sacrifices, a priest of secret rites"

But neither the Senate decrees nor the threat of harsh penalties prevented the Roman and Etruscan libertines from pursuing the worst debauchery. The Roman historian Livy tells us that these Bacchic rites were first introduced to Etruria, then to Rome, by a "nameless Greek."

"A nameless Greek," Livy writes, "came first to Etruria, possessed of none of those many arts which the Greek people, supreme as it is in learning, brought to us

1. *The full text of this law is quoted by Albert Camoy,* Dictionnaire de la mythologie gréco-romaine *(Brussels: Paul Guethner, n.d.).*

in numbers for the cultivation of mind and body, but a dabbler in sacrifices and a fortune-teller; nor was he one who, by frankly disclosing his creed and publicly proclaiming both his profession and his system, filled minds with error, but a priest of secret rites performed by night. These were initiatory rites which at first were imparted to a few, then began to be generally known among men and women. To the religious element in them were added the delights of wine and feasts, that the minds of a larger number might be attracted. When wine had inflamed their minds, and night and the mingling of males with females, youth with aged, had destroyed every sentiment of modesty, all varieties of corruption first began to be practiced, since each one had at hand the pleasure answering to the one to which his nature was most inclined. There was not one form of vice alone, the promiscuous matings of free men and women, but perjured witnesses, forged seals and wills and evidence, all issued from this same workshop: likewise poisonings and murders of kindred, so that at times not even the bodies were found for burial. Much was ventured by craft, more by violence. This violence was concealed because amid the howlings and the crash of drums and cymbals no cry of the sufferers could be heard as the debauchery and murders proceeded.

"The destructive power of this evil spread from Etruria to Rome like the contagion of a pestilence. At first the size of the city, with abundant room and tolerance for such evils, concealed it."(1)

1. Livy, *Bk. XXXIX, 8-9 (pp. 241-243)*.

Bloody orgies along the Tiber

Livy then relates the story of a young man who, nearly killed during one of these Bacchic celebrations, miraculously managed to escape his attackers.

"Men, as if insane, with fanatical tossings of their bodies, would utter prophecies. Matrons in the dress of Bacchantes, with dishevelled hair and carrying blazing torches, would run down to the Tiber, and plunging their torches into the water (because they contained live sulphur mixed with calcium) would bring them out still burning. Men were alleged to have been carried off by the gods who had been bound to a machine and borne away out of sight to hidden caves: they were those who had refused either to conspire or to join in the crimes or to suffer abuse. Their number was very great, almost constituting a second state; among them were certain men and women of high rank" (Bk. XXXIX, 13; p. 255).

Theopompus' slanderous gossip

The Greek historian Theopompus, nicknamed, as noted earlier, the "worst of gossips," claimed that these scandalous events had always been a prominent feature of Etruscan history. In a notorious text transcribed word for word by the Greek grammarian Athenaeus (c. A.D. 200) in his *Learned Banquet*, he paints for posterity a frightful portrait of Etruscan mores. Especially fond of scabrous tales and spicy gossip, Theopompus depicts the Etruscans as antiquity's most depraved, most immoral, and most irreligious people. Athenaeus writes:

"Theopompus says that the Tyrrhenians possess their women in common; these take great care of their bodies and exercise naked, often along with men, sometimes among themselves; for it is not shameful for them to show themselves naked. They sit down to table not beside their own husbands but beside any of the guests, and they even drink to the health of anyone they please. Moreover they are great wine-bibbers and very beautiful to behold. The Tyrrhenians bring up together all those children that are born to them, heedless of who their father may be. These children live in the same manner as their protectors, passing the most of their time in drinking and having commerce with all the women indifferently. There is no shame for a Tyrrhenian to be seen committing a sexual act in public or indeed submitting to it, for this too is a custom of the country. And so removed are they from regarding the act as shameful that when the master of the house is engaged in making love and he is being called they say: 'He is doing so-and-so,' referring to the act quite impudently by its name."

"When there are gatherings of family or friends, this is how they do: first of all, when they have finished drinking and are ready for bed and while the torches are still lighted the servants bring in sometimes courtesans, sometimes handsome boys, sometimes their own wives. When they have taken their pleasure of the women or the men, they make strapping young fellows lie with the latter. They make love and pursue their pleasures in full view of everyone, but usually surround their couches with small frames of woven branches over which they drape their cloaks. They certainly have much commerce with women, but they always enjoy themselves much better with boys and young men. The latter are in this country quite beautiful to behold, for they live lives of ease and their bodies are hairless. Moreover, all the barbarians who live towards the west cover their bodies with wax and shave themselves; and among the Tyrrhenians there are even many establishments and practicians for this purpose, as common as barbers in our own land. When they go there they lend themselves to the work without reserve, without having any shame of being seen, even by passers-by." (1)

Mezentius, king of Caere, and his barbarous tortures

In his scathing description of Etruscan mores, the Greek historian seems to have intentionally ignored the outstanding qualities of this people. Livy wrote that "the Etruscan communities, deeply learned as they were in sacred lore of all kinds, were more concerned than any other nation with religious matters" (Bk. V, 1; p. 325). These communities were actually contaminated only belatedly, precisely when their famous "discipline," a model of severity, was falling into disuse. Hence Claudius' speech and his appeals to restore the college of the haruspices, a last bastion against moral laxity and decadence. Theopompus also

1. *As quoted by Jacques Heurgon in* Daily Life of the Etruscans*, p. 34.*

fails to mention that the deadly seeds that contaminated the Etruscan and Roman spirit were sown by the Greeks and the Orientals.

In reality, there are historical reasons for the systematically scandalous portrait drawn by Theopompus. The Greeks never forgot the terrible struggle that, for many centuries, had pitted them against the Etruscans and their allies, the Carthaginians. The outcome of this struggle was vital for both of them: control of the western Mediterranean was at stake. The Etruscans had also opposed expansion by the Greek colonists of southern Italy, and Etruscan pirates had terrorized the entire Italian coast and threatened the Greek ports established in that area. There had also been the Famous sea battle of Alalia off the Corsican coast, where the Greek prisoners captured by the Etruscans suffered a horrible fate by order of Mezentius, the cruel king of Caere, as Virgil states:

Why call to mind his hideous holocausts?
His unspeakable misdeeds?—may all the gods
Serve him and his family likewise—why he would even
Bind living men to the dead, lashed hand to hand
And face to face—could one conceive of such a
                                                            [torture?—
And in the corruption and running filth of this
Appalling embrace do them to lingering death. (1)

1. *Virgil,* The Aeneid, *trans. Patric Dickinson, Bk. VIII (p. 183). Virgil's passage was cited by Basil Modestov,* Introduction à l'histoire romaine *(Paris: Alcan, 1907). This work, with an introduction by Salomon Reinach, explains at length how their Etruscan heritage was a decisive factor in the emergence and spread of Roman genius.*

Such atrocities had certainly left indelible memories among the Greeks. In large measure this explains Theopompus' overly slanderous remarks.

Posidonius, the Syrian philosopher, visits Etruria

It would be well to compare these libidinous slanders with the testimony of Posidonius of Apamea who, at the end of the second century B.C., had returned from his extensive scholarly travels in the West with a more fair-minded appraisal of Etruscan mores. While Theopompus is but a mediocre, scandal-mongering compiler, Posidonius is an exceptionally distinguished philosopher.

Born in Syria, he left his homeland at an early age. He taught at Rhodes, where Cicero and Pompey were among his students, and traveled far and wide in Greece, Egypt and, in particular, Italy, where he lingered for a long time. He was a keen observer of Roman society and became friendly with a number of Etruscan personalities from Rome who took him to visit several Etruscan cities.(1) To be sure, the Stoic philosopher had little tolerance for moral laxity, which he harshly condemned. But he was perceptive enough to differentiate between a few degenerate elements, which exist everywhere, and the rest of Etruscan society which, as a general rule, remained very wholesome. His assessment is well balanced: though

1. *On Posidonius and the Etruscans, see Marcel Renard's well-researched article in* Hommages à Albert Grenier *(Brussels:* Latomus, *1962).*

he praises the Etruscans' courage, their religious discipline, and their enterprise, he severely criticizes their taste for indolence and luxury. He reports both vices and virtues with the same concern for truth.

Etruscans, masters in science, letters, and theology

Here is Posidonius' text as handed down to us by Diodorus Siculus:

"The Etruscans, who formerly were distinguished for their energy, conquered a vast territory and there founded many important towns. They also disposed of powerful naval forces and for a long time enjoyed mastery of the seas, so much so that the one which washed the western shores of Italy was called by them the Tyrrhenian. They perfected the equipment of their land forces by inventing what is called the trumpet, which is of the greatest utility in war and was named by them Tyrrhenian; they also devised marks of honor for the generals who led them, assigning to them lictors, an ivory throne, and a toga bordered with purple. And in their houses they invented the peristyle, which is a great convenience in that it deadens the uproar caused by their great crowds of servants. The majority of these discoveries were imitated by the Romans, who perfected them and introduced them into their civilization. They encouraged the progress of letters, science, nature, and theology and developed to a higher degree than any other people the interpretation of thunder. This is why today they still inspire those who are masters of nearly all the world (that is to say, the Romans) with such deep admiration, and why they are employed today as interpreters of the celestial signs."

Sumptuously dressed tables, delicate living

Following this legitimate praise of Etruria, Posidonius described the way of life there, an opulent life thanks to the unusual fertility of its soil. This, the philosopher Posidonius thought, was the root cause of Etruscan decadence. In this overly mild climate the Etruscans had lost the strength for which their ancestors had been praised.

"As they inhabit a land fertile in fruits of all kinds and cultivate it assiduously, they enjoy an abundance of agricultural produce which not only is sufficient for themselves but by its excess leads them to unbridled luxury and indolence. For twice a day they have tables sumptuously dressed and laid with everything that can contribute towards delicate living; they have coverings embroidered with flowers and are served wine in quantities of silver bowls, and they have at their call a considerable number of slaves. Some of the latter are of a rare beauty; others dress themselves in clothes more magnificent than befits their station of servitude, and the domestic staff have all kinds of private dwellings: as indeed do most of the freed men. In general they have abandoned the valiant steadfastness that they prized so much in former days, and by their indulgence in banquets and effeminate delights they have lost the reputation which their ancestors won in war, which does not surprise us. But what served more than anything to turn them to soft and idle living was the quality of the land, for, living in a country that produces everything and is of inexhaustible fecundity, they are able to store up large quantities of fruit of every kind. Etruria is indeed very fertile, extending for the most part over plains separated by hills with arable slopes, and it is moderately well-watered, not only in the winter season, but also during the summer." (1)

"Long life to you! you belly-gods!"

Indolence, a love of luxury and good food: these are the words most often repeated by Latin and Greek historians in their description of the Etruscans, grown fat and obese. Catullus, in evoking the various peoples of Italy, reserves a special place, between the "skinflint Umbrian" and the "swarthy and buck-toothed Lanuvian," for the "plump Etruscan." Virgil describes a sacrifice accompanied by flute music: "while near the altars a fat Tyrrhenian blew ivory pipes." Cato, the touchy critic of Roman morals, vilified certain Etruscan civil servants who had grown corpulent: "How can the state benefit from a body when the whole area between the throat and the waist is taken up by the abdomen?" As for the satiric poet Lucilius, he heaps scorn on the Etruscan upper class, calling them "gluttons, guzzlers and gourmandizers who stuffed their bellies with lard and sides of pork, gorged themselves on tender

1. *Diodorus Siculus, Bk. V, 40, as quoted by Heurgon,* Daily Life of the Etruscans, *pp. 36-37.*

asparagus and cauliflower, and destroyed themselves with lobster and gigantic sturgeon." The poet concludes his diatribe with this stinging barb: "Long life to you! you belly-gods!" Another satirist, Laelius, sings the praises of vegetarian frugality which he contrasts to the dietary debauchery of the Etruscans and maintains that the gourmandizing "so common among the inhabitants of Etruria" is incompatible with an alert and subtle mind. "How can those whose hearts are filled with mud and wine be wise?"

This distressing reputation of the Etruscans appears not only in literary texts, of which we have just cited a few examples; there is also archeological evidence that confirms this image of an Etruscan people devoted to indolence, debauchery, and gluttony. The funerary frescoes of Vulci, Caere, and Tarquinia abound in scenes of banquets and reveling. A statue which stands today in the Museum of Florence depicts an obese Etruscan (which is, moreover, the title ascribed to the terracotta itself). And what does he look like? We see a large sack of flesh spread before us with an innocent look on his face. A garland of flowers is hanging from his shoulders and he is nonchalantly holding an immense wine cup at the end of his right arm. He wears a large ring on the third finger of his left hand. But what is most striking is the character's belly—an enormous, round belly displaying a big bare navel!

The political and religious reasons for Etruscan decadence

A question often raised is how this profoundly religious people who had shown such courage and daring and who had created Italy's first and most brilliant civilization, came to decline into such decadence? For, even if we do not lend much credence to Theopompus and his calumny, Etruscan morals had in fact grown lax. There is, as we have noted, the explanation given by Posidonius: the fertility of Etruscan soil. However, it seems that other more profound causes precipitated this decadence. As always, these reasons are religious and political. We have emphasized how Etruscan religion was essentially fatalist. According to the *Libri rituales*, or the long-lost ritual books, the duration of the Etruscan nation was predetermined with unrelenting fatality to be ten centuries. And we know, owing especially to Massimo Pallottino's scholarly research, that Etruscan chronology begins in the tenth century B.C.—in 968 B.C., to be precise.

"Just as the individual could guard himself against destiny by means of sacrifices," writes this eminent Etruscologist, "the nation itself also had the opportunity, during the first ten centuries of its time-span, to protect itself against the blows of fate .... But the existence of the Etruscan people, as a distinct ethnic entity, never went beyond the limits that the Tyrrhenians had imposed upon themselves .... This submission to fatality explains the attitude of the Etruscans of the late periods: their disappearance was ineluctable, forever predetermined, and any attempt to change the course of destiny would have been vain."

Most of the archeological and literary sources cited above have to do precisely with these "Etruscans of the late period," that is, with those Etruscans who lived during the final periods of their history, after which there was supposed to be only nothingness and death. The fat Etruscan in the Museum of Naples, who probably lived during the second or first century B.C., was probably keenly aware of the death inexorably awaiting his own nation. Heir to a glorious but distant past, reduced to bondage by Rome, knowing that the "end of time" was near, the fat man from Naples abandoned himself to the unbridled pursuit of table pleasures—the last pleasures that Roman power had granted the leading citizens of Etruria without balking.

A Nazi ideologue criticizes the Etruscans

Twenty centuries later, Rome's "tolerance" of the Etruscans was sharply criticized by the Nazi ideologue Alfred Rosenberg in his book *The Myth of the 20th Century* (1930). As Rosenberg considered the Romans to be Indo-Europeans—which has been acknowledged —and the Etruscans to be a mysterious Semitic tribe originating from the farthest reaches of Asia, he denied the value of the Etruscan heritage and maintained that Etruscan civilization, and above all its religion, hastened Roman decadence. For, in Rosenberg's eyes, Etruria was nothing other than a "Judeo-Semitic" center which Rome should have destroyed with the utmost energy.

"Rome," he writes, "was founded by a northern wave, long before the Germans and the Gauls had spread across the fertile valleys of the Southern Alps and put an end to domination by the Etruscans, this mysterious foreign people from primitive Asia.

"The Romans represent Nordic blood but the Etruscans, who populated part of Italy before the arrival of the Romans, represent Asiatic blood ....

"The horrible orgies of the Bacchanalia, as well as the entire array of magic and sorcery, owe their existence to the Etruscans.

"In short, the Etruscans poisoned Roman blood and transmitted their imaginary world of torments in the hereafter to the Christian Church. These infamous superstitions bequeathed to the Middle Ages by the Etruscan spirit must be discarded. Then the Roman Church, which is forever tied to the torments of the Etruscan underworld, will crumble just as completely."

This Nazi ideologue's latter claim, the legacy of Etruscan superstitions to the Christian Church and the Middle-Ages, is even more phantasmagoric than the Semitism of the Etruscans, which remains to be proven.

4

THE
RESURRECTION
OF ETRURIA

"The fear of death intensifies the pleasures of life."

Vauvenargues

As a political power in Italy the Etruscan nation had virtually vanished by the first century A.D. This nation, which had once struck fear in the peoples of Italy, became a Roman province. As the colonies created by Imperial Rome flourished, the ancient Etruscan *lucumonies* declined, succumbing to their mortal fate. The Etruscan empire and its grandeur were nothing but a distant memory and there remained of some Etruscan metropolises only a heap of ruins overrun by weeds . . . .

The Latin poet Propertius gives a poignant description of one of these cities, Veii, Rome's neighbor and secular rival, a description which also held true for Caere, Tarquinia, and many other Etruscan cities. The ancient and prestigious Etruria was nothing but an immense desolate landscape where occasionally one could see the remains of a few forgotten necropolises.

> *Ancient Veii,*
> *what a kingdom you were then with your golden throne*
> *set up in the marketplace. Now the leisurely music*
> *of the shepherd's horn sounds within your walls,*
> *and over your bones they go harvesting.* (1)

Immense wealth awaited the excavator's pick

At the beginning of the nineteenth century, as we have noted, the desolate panorama of these ancient Etruscan cities was unchanged—dead cities, clusters of abandoned ruins in the midst of fields, vast cemeteries choked with weeds.

The discovery of the Vulci necropolis in 1828 radically altered this situation. The art objects, jewelry, and immense wealth brought to light provided substantial new source material for Etruscan archeology. Interest in this civilization was rekindled, prompting a rush of archeologists, scholars, and diggers of all kinds to the area. Soon, previously unknown names became familiar to all who, for more or less commendable reasons, had gone in search of the buried treasures of the ancient Etruscans. Because of the variety, wealth, and size of the remains that were discovered, Vulci,

1. The Poems of Propertius, *Bk. IV, 10 (p. 226).*

Caere, and Tarquinia represent the first stages of an inspiring adventure that is still in progress—a resurrection.

"The history of Etruscan studies," writes Massimo Pallottino, "is closely linked to the story of the resurrection of the dead cities of Etruria. For more than two centuries now, investigators of all kinds, impalled at first by greed for treasure, simple curiosity, or interest in local history and only later by scientific motives, have quarried relentlessly at the remains of the great Etruscan cities and cemeteries. Nevertheless, anyone who is familiar with the Etruscan countryside knows that an incalculable amount of evidence needed for the reconstruction of its ancient civilization still lies below ground awaiting excavation." (1)

The moving discovery of the "François Tomb"

Beginning in the nineteenth century, the resurrection of Etruria has had a history at once varied, provocative, and dramatic.

Lacking in technical resources, often racing with treasure-hunters, the archeologists of the nineteenth century, by their tenacity and courage, loom as veritable pioneers. Examples of this group were the Tuscan A. François and the Frenchman Noël des Vergers, both of whom were to die of malaria contracted during excavations in the unhealthy region of Maremma, near Vulci.

1. *Massimo Pallottino,* The Etruscans, *p. 105.*

In a voluminous work on Etruscan civilization,(1) Noël des Vergers describes the inexpressible emotion that seized him when he first discovered the Vulci Tomb, later called the François Tomb in memory of his Tuscan companion. The explorer narrates:

"When the stone closing the entranceway to the crypt gave way at the last blow of the pick and the blaze of our torches lit vaults whose silence and darkness had remained undisturbed for more than twenty centuries, I was awed by the spectacle spread before my eyes. Everything was in the same condition as on the day when the entrance had been walled in, and we saw ancient Etruria as it had appeared during its greatness. Reclining on their funeral couches, warriors dressed in armor seemed to be resting after having given battle to the Romans and our ancestors, the Gauls. Shapes, clothing, fabrics, colors appeared for a few minutes and then everything vanished as the outside air penetrated the tomb, where at first our sputtering torches had threatened to go out. It was an evocation of the past that lasted scarcely the time of a dream and vanished as if to punish us for our reckless curiosity."

Underground on all fours

The Tuscan archeologist François shares with us his participation in a fascinating and sometimes dangerous adventure, the exploration of a tomb at this period:

1. *Noël des Vergers, L'Etrurie et les Etrusques, 2 vols., 1862-1864.* Cited by R. Bianchi Bandinelli and A. Giuliano, Etruschi e Italici prima del dominio di Roma.

"Disregarding the danger of a sudden landslide or a caving in," he wrote in his report on the exploration of the labyrinth in Chiusi, "I crawled into its underground area on all fours through an extremely small opening which I discovered by chance near the walls of modern Chiusi, taking as my sole companion one of my workers, a loyal and intrepid man, whom I had provided with a light and chains to save us if any accident occurred because of our efforts. But imagine my astonishment when, after having traveled the length of the corridor (which was three Florentine fathoms wide) on all fours and dug into the rock, I realized that the earth which blocked it three fathoms above continued uninterrupted. For me it was additional proof that this place was a tomb, for had it been built for any other human purpose it would have been useless to fill it up with earth." (1)

Science and technology in the service of archeology

The richest Etruscan tombs were brought to light with the first excavations. But the unearthed remains— art objects, frescoes, jewelry—often were neither catalogued nor examined with the necessary care and according to proper scientific methods. Even fabulous

1. Bulletin de l'Institut de correspondance archéologique, *1849. The archeologist François was a tireless explorer who was present at all the Tuscan sites in the middle of the 19th century. His greatest claim to fame was the discovery of one of the richest necropolises of Vulci, a necropolis which now bears the name François Tomb.*

treasures sometimes disappeared into the hands of common treasure-hunters.

It was not until modern times that museums and scholarly societies took control of the situation. Thanks to technical progress, Etruscan archeology then took a decisive step forward. Today technical advances are being applied in the three major phases of archeological excavation: prospecting, exploration, and conservation.

The first phase, prospecting the terrain, is probably the most exciting archeological stage.

Prospecting the terrain means detecting the vestiges of ancient constructions buried long ago beneath the ground. The Etruscan vestiges are essentially tombs, sometimes making up vast necropolises covering hundreds of acres. Aerial photography is one recent technique by which the layout of these necropolises may be rapidly, and often precisely, determined:

"Air photography," writes the French archeologist Raymond Bloch, "has made it possible to establish the general layout of the great cemetery areas, for the *tumuli* (1) which originally covered the tombs appear in the form of whitish patches standing out from the surrounding soil.... On a darker background of cultivated ground we see a scatter of white patches, the remains of the leveled tumuli. The arrangement and layout of the tombs are clearly shown, for cutting through the apparent confusion of the countless white circles we can follow the line of the great funeral roads, the *vie sepolcrali*, round which was organized and

1. Tumulus, *pl.* tumuli: *large earthen mounds or cone-shaped constructions that the Ancients erected above their tombs.*

developed over the centuries the densely packed pattern of the tombs." (1)

Electric probes, periscopes and chemical analyses

A method now available to archeologists in the second phase of their work, field research, is an electrical detection device called the potentiometer. This easy-to-operate instrument measures the variations in the electrical resistance of the ground and calls the attention of the excavator to the possible existence of archeological remains underground. (2)

Once the presence of the tomb or monument has been detected, the size and value of the discovered ruins must be assessed by the archeologist before he actually begins excavation. Electrical probes are used for this preliminary exploration of the Etruscan tombs.

1. *Bloch,* The Ancient Civilization of the Etruscans, *p. 132. This technique was used for the first time in 1947 by the English archeologist John Bradford, who carefully studied photographs taken for strategic purposes by the Royal Air Force during World War II in Italy. The results of John Bradford's studies on the application of aerial photography to archeological research were published for the first time in 1947 in the English review* Antiquity *("Etruria From the Air," vol. 21, p. 74), and the technique has been widely used ever since. Moreover, a center of archeological air photography has recently been founded in Rome.*
2. *The earth is known to store electricity. The conductivity of the earth in a given area is affected by the presence of brickworks, cavities, tombs, or trenches, changes which are registered by the potentiometer. Quite recently (June 1975) the buried foundations of a Romanesque church were discovered in the vicinity of La Charité-sur-Loire with the help of the potentiometer.*

A hole from 4 to 10 inches in diameter is bored through the relatively thin layer of soil above the tomb and then through the ceiling of the tomb itself. A periscope fastened to the tip of the probe is inserted into the chamber of the tomb, enabling the archeologist to examine its contents at leisure. This procedure has at least two advantages : a considerable amount of time is saved and any risks of deterioration as a result of overly rough drilling or, in the case of delicate frescoes, sudden contact with the outside air, are eliminated.

There are, of course, modern techniques for the third phase of archeological work, the conservation of these vestiges. These are, for the most part, chemical procedures which are used not only in Etruscology but in many other archeological fields. We will not examine them at length as they are too complex and require a full understanding of chemistry. It is enough to say that they constitute a valuable contribution to the conservation of frescoes and funeral paintings in Etruscan necropolises.

Recent discoveries increasing at a rapid pace

Since the modern methods noted above began to be applied systematically, discoveries have been increasing rapidly in Tuscany. Raymond Bloch presents an impressive report on the digging expeditions carried out in the years 1956 to 1959 :

"In the course of a single campaign of ten months in 1956-57, Lerici's team from the Polytechnic Institute of Milan identified 500 new tombs. Many of these, of course, had already been entered and despoiled of most of their contents, but in spite of this the campaign yielded some thousands of Etruscan, Italic, and Greek objects which have enriched the resources of the Villa Giulia Museum. In 1958-59 the same team tackled the necropolis of Tarquinia. Here no new painted tomb had been discovered for 66 years, the last one being the Tomb of the Bulls, found in 1894. In eighteen months' work by the Lerici team a thousand new tombs were identified. These included, in 1958, a number of painted tombs of the first importance—the Tombs of the Olympiad, the Ship, the Mouse, the Red Lions, the Jade Lions, and the Skull; and in 1959 three further painted tombs. Since then the pace of discovery has scarcely slackened; and indeed the mass of new finds is beginning to raise problems of study and of publication."(1)

Tuscan painters—Braque and Rouault

It is impossible to recount in detail the innumerable digging expeditions that have gone on for a century and a half and that every day yield valuable information promoting a better understanding of mysterious Etruria. It would be a gargantuan task entailing many volumes. Nevertheless, it is possible to bring up a few of the important archeological discoveries that have provided an indispensable introduction to this incomparably refined art, the art of the Etruscans.

1. *Raymond Bloch,* The Ancient Civilization of the Etruscans, *pp. 134-135.*

Here again we are mainly concerned with funerary discoveries. Sometimes buried dozens of yards beneath Tuscan soil, the Etruscan necropolises have preserved intact masterpieces that are valuable testimony to a once brilliant civilization and a remarkable way of life and death. These masterpieces never cease to dazzle and fascinate us by their artistic richness, variety, and astounding modernity as well. The bare tormented style and violent aggressive colors of some paintings inevitably bring to mind Braque, Kandinsky, and even certain "hyperrealists" such as Sloane, Mintho, or Grotewöl.(1) Had Tuscan painters already experienced the same anguish, the same fears as our contemporaries? Is there not a secret link between certain ochre-colored frescoes of Tarquinia, imbued with a sense of gripping tragedy, and certain Rouault canvases bathed in painful mystery? Despite the twenty-five centuries separating us from puzzling Etruria, its art is akin to our own. And though we do not as yet know its language, each statue unearthed, each fresco, each painting speaks to us in a language we know.

Originality and importance of Etruscan art

Before surveying a few Tuscan necropolises it seems appropriate to emphasize how different Etruscan art is from Greek art, despite the assertions of

1. *In 1966, this writer devoted a film to Braque and Rouault entitled* Le Regard du peintre *(The Painter's Gaze).*

certain art historians, Willy Zschietzschmann in particular, to the contrary.(1) This noted professor at the University of Giessen, who has devoted truly excellent works to Greek art, has attempted to reduce Etruscan art to a mere offshoot of Hellenic art, following, in that respect, the hastily elaborated theories of nineteenth century archeologists and historians. Fortunately, such injustices have been corrected by the respected Etruscologist Massimo Pallottino who, after many years of painstaking and unbiased research, acknowledges the profound originality of Etruscan art, an art that we have found to be much closer to modern art than is Greek art with its highly civilized proportions. To be sure, Tuscan artists were in certain respects inspired by Greek art. But these were merely superficial derivations that in no manner detracted from their powerful, expressive originality.

"Nineteenth-century critics," writes Pallottino, "largely dominated by classical or naturalistic preconceptions, tended on the whole to answer this question in the negative. For them, Etruscan productions were to be regarded as provincial manifestations of Greek art, crude and aesthetically valueless. All finds of any value made in Etruria were at once attributed to Greek artists. But the new directions taken by art history and aesthetic criticism at the beginning of the twentieth century allowed full validity of expression to artistic experiences outside the classical orbit and opened the way to the comprehension of stylistic

1. *Willy Zschietzschmann,* Etrusques, Rome *(Paris : Payot, n.d.). This work is the sixth volume of the series "Histoire de l'Art" edited by Y. Brunhammer.*

phenomena of the ancient world that had hitherto been
misjudged, as in the case of the artistic production
of Etruria." (1)

"A raggedness of edge and a certain wildness of light and shade"

D.H. Lawrence holds the same view. In his wonder-
ful book, *Etruscan Places*, the English novelist is an
incomparable guide for lovers of Etruscan art. Free of
esthetic or historical prejudice, he cast a fresh glance at
Etruscan masterpieces, as he himself asserted. His
constant concern was to avoid the historical stereo-
types so detrimental to true knowledge: "After having
read all the learned suggestions, most of them
contradicting one another; and then having looked
sensitively at the tombs and the Etruscan things that are
left, one must accept one's own resultant feeling . . . .
The Etruscans are not a theory or a thesis. If they are
anything, they are an experience." Earlier in his book
Lawrence writes: "Most people despise everything
B.C. that isn't Greek, for the good reason that it ought to
be Greek if it isn't. So Etruscan things are put down as
a feeble Graeco-Roman imitation" (p. 9).

After a visit to the Museum of Volterra, to see the
vestiges of the very luxurious tomb of the Caecina
family, decorated with Greek-looking mythological
motifs, Lawrence exclaimed:

"Most curious these 'classic' subjects: so un-

1. *Pallottino*, The Etruscans, *pp. 166-167.*

classic! ... The Greek and Roman "boiled" sort of form gives way to a raggedness of edge and a certain wildness of light and shade which promises the later Gothic, but which is still held down by the heavy mysticism from the East" (p. 180).

The rise and fall of Caere

The Caere necropolis remains the best and the most eloquent introduction to Etruscan art which, despite a few derivations, differs so greatly from Greek and Roman productions. The richness of this necropolis—the profusion of art works, articles, and tombs—is truly unusual. We can still feel the heartbeat of Etruria pulsing through its tumuli, sarcophagi, frescoes, and household utensils.

Cerveteri, a small village about 25 miles from Rome, is all that remains of the ancient Etruscan city. South of this village, an immense field of ruins from the necropolis covers an area of many acres, ruins that scarcely evoke Caere's former splendor.

Rome's formidable rival for many centuries, Caere was a prosperous city thanks, above all, to its metal-rich territories of Tolfa and Allumiere near the city itself. Caere was a metalworking center and had many workshops where skilled craftsmen worked in bronze, gold, and silver, carving admirable ivories and producing the finest ceramic ware of the western Mediterranean. Thanks to its three ports, the largest of which was Pyrgi, Caere maintained trade relations with all the

Mediterranean countries.(1) But the serious political and economic crises of the fifth century were to strike a fatal blow to Caere and other Etruscan cities. The rivalries that pitted Etruscans, Greeks, and Carthaginians against each other for control of the western Mediterranean exacted its toll on Caere. Weakened, deprived of its fleet after several defeats at sea, Caere survived as best it could. After a long period of decline, it fell into the hands of Roman troops in 273 B.C. and became an insignificant provincial city whose fate was later to be sealed by malaria.

"The history of Caere," writes Sibylle von Cles-Reden, "can be clearly read in the shadow of its substance—the City of the Dead .... Caere's zenith is reflected in the gigantic dimensions of the tombs of this epoch. Never are more than twelve members of a single family found in their last resting-place in these chambers, embedded deep in the tufa-stone foundations of the mounds. But later, when the star of Caere begins to wane, the monuments become gradually more modest. They give way gradually to chamber-tombs carved out at the foot of the tumuli along the streets that intersect the necropolis. In the period of the Tyrrhenian nation's decline, there is a certain anxiety about the way the name and origins of the deceased are put on record, as though the Etruscans were already becoming uneasily aware of how completely their race might be forgotten."(2)

1. *We have already noted the discovery, at Pyrgi, of a bilingual document bearing a dual inscription in Punic and Etruscan.*
2. *Sybille von Cles-Reden,* The Buried People, *p. 31.*

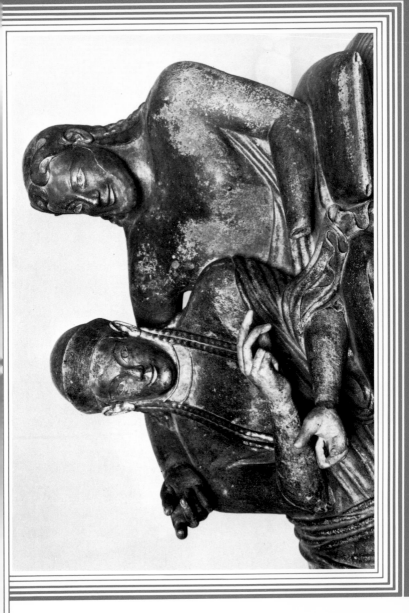

Detail of a terracotta sarcophagus: husband and wife on funeral couch. From Cerveteri. About 530 B.C. Louvre, Paris. *(Bulloz)*

Painted dish with a figure of a fighting elephant and its little one. Third centu[ry]
Villa Giulia Museum, Rome. *(Giraudon)*

A splendor beyond all imagining

It was only in 1836 that the excavation initiated a few years earlier began to bear fruit. That was the very year when Father Regolini and General Galassi unearthed a tomb dating back to the seventh century B.C. in a vineyard located outside the necropolis.(1) Named in honor of those who discovered it, the Regolini-Galassi Tomb has provided Etruscologists with an abundant yield of artwork and articles of all kinds, which are now kept in the Gregorian Etruscan Museum of the Vatican.

"With the discovery of the Regolini-Galassi Tomb," writes Claude Boncompain, "the image of primitive Etruscan civilization shone with a previously unsuspected brilliance .... In the first chamber was the cadaver of a man lying on a bronze bed; in the second, the corpse of a richly dressed woman .... This was probably a noble couple .... In contrast to the simplicity and austerity that characterized the previous epochs, the splendor displayed by the Etruscans is beyond all imagining .... Adorned like a goddess, the woman wears a round pendant, a gold leaf decorated with incised motifs: remarkably executed animals and plants."(2)

The author then emphasizes the exceptional skill of the Tuscan goldsmiths and the stupendous richness of

1. *Father Regoloni and General Galassi were the faithful correspondents of the famous Etruscan Academy of Cortona, mentioned at the beginning of this work.*
2. *Claude Boncompain,* Lucienne et les Etrusques *(Paris: Albin Michel, 1951). This short fictionalized account lacks neither charm nor taste; though it makes no claim to great scholarship, it is an excellent guide to Etruscan antiquities.*

their work. Few people of Antiquity ever attained such mastery in the art of jewelry and only recently have German jewelers rediscovered certain Etruscan techniques.

The secrets of the Tuscan jewelers

The jewels discovered in the Regolini-Galassi Tomb and many other tombs do indeed constitute an inestimable treasure: diadems, ear pendants, simple necklaces, double or triple necklaces with drops, chains and braids which hang from the shoulders and cross the chest and reach as far as the hips, plaited belts, bracelets and armbands, rings for both hands, all the fingers, and even the various joints as if the entire contents of the deceased's jewel box were spread upon his effigy. (1)

The widest variety of materials was used by the Tuscan jewelers: bronze, silver, iron, amber. To these various elements one must add beaver bones and teeth, out of which somewhat crude incrustations were fashioned; shells that were pierced to turn them into pendants; certain hard stones, the remains of weapons and utensils from the Stone Age, which had been piously conserved as amulets; figurines of varnished earthenware imported from the Orient, to which certain preservative powers were ascribed and which were hung like shells on necklace strings; pieces of uncut or

1. *Some of these jewels were displayed in Paris in 1965 at the Louvre's major Etruscan Art Exhibition.*

worked ivory; and finally, precious gems used as ring-stones and set in the gold of bracelets, earrings, and pendants.

But it is the gold jewelry above all that made the Tuscan jewelers famous.

Without going into any great detail on the methods used by these jewelers, suffice it to say that of all the gold jewelry uncovered in Etruria, the most interesting articles from the technical standpoint are those involving filigree work and granulation. Filigree work is a technique which consists of fashioning gold into thin filaments, often as slender as a human hair. Sometimes these filaments are braided or linked to make chains or ribbons. Sometimes they are curved, rolled, and bent into openwork motifs. And sometimes they are soldered onto a surface and, in light relief, are shaped into various patterns: meanders, interlaced ribbons, scrolls, rosettes, palm leaves, circles, and animal figures. (1)

As for granulation, it is an even more delicate technique than filigree work. It involves a countless number of minute spheroidal gold grains, almost invisible to the naked eye and only clearly observable with a magnifying glass, which are so closely pressed together thay they form a uniform surface slightly rough to the touch.

A remarkable example of this Etruscan gold jewelry

1. *This technique may be clearly observed on a beautiful disk probably coming from a brooch, now in the Louvre. At the center is a flower-work of curved lamellae with a ribbing of tiny droplets. The surrounding flowers are each made up of a sphere set onto a network of gold-wired rings that simulate petals.*

consists of a necklace pendant representing the horned head of the river-god Achelous, found in Orvieto. The entire bear and crown are of granulated gold, whereas the curls of his hair are made of filigree spirals with gold droplets in the middle.

Secrets not rediscovered until 1964

Before German jewelers discovered the secrets of these techniques in 1964, the methods used by the Etruscans to obtain such a surface of gold grains remained unknown for many centuries. The nineteenth-century masters of Roman jewelry, the Castellani brothers, had sought the solution of this difficult problem for many years. They had performed thousands of experiments, had tried all sorts of chemical agents, and had traveled into the middle of the Apennines to look for workers in distant villages where the traditions of the ancient techniques apparently had survived. But they had only partially succeeded in reproducing Etruscan granulation. Their method consisted of aiming the flame of a blowtorch at imperceptible particles of gold which would melt into bubbles; glue was applied in advance to the surface to be covered. Particles of gold dust were scattered upon it and soldered on using a flux of arsenic acid salt. The jewelry thus obtained was truly remarkable, but however delicate this granulated surface may have appeared, it lacked the fineness of the ancient granulation work. The Castellani brothers had openly acknowledged this themselves.

"We are convinced," they said, "that the ancients

possessed some chemical method that we do not know, for despite all our efforts, we have not managed to reproduce the exquisite delicacy of some of these works, a delicacy that we have given up all hope of ever achieving unless new scientific discoveries are made."(1)

The puzzle of the Caere hydriae

In addition to these superb jewels, the Regolini-Galassi Tomb yielded admirably decorated furniture and utensils: hemispheric bronze cauldrons adorned with fantastic animal heads on their rims and placed on top of high tripods; round decorative shields: cups in embossed silver; a bed, a kind of bronze grill raised up on six feet and including a headboard; large vases containing wheat, oil, honey, and eggs for the deceased; as well as many other smaller bronze and terracotta vessels. All these vases, testimony to the very rich production of Etruscan ceramists, are painted in the most vivid and shimmering colors: red, black, mauve, bright yellow. Dubbed the "hydriae of Caere" because of their shape, these vases arouse lively debates among art historians who still wonder whether they are Etruscan or Greek. G.A. Mansuelli, author of a remarkable work to which we referred earlier, thinks these hydriae may be attributed to Greek artists working in the shops of Caere.

"The problem of these painted vases," writes

1. *Statement made to the Academie des Inscriptions, December 20, 1860.*

Mansuelli, "within the black-figure technique, yet with abundant polychrome notes, is one of the most warmly discussed in Etruscan Archaism : with the layout of the scenes generally spacious and well-balanced, the color construction closely related to that of original Ionic pottery, both technique and taste in decorative elements soon suggested that these might be the work of Greek craftsmen, whilst the possibility has been expressed, because of some realistic and caricatural features, that they may be local productions. The thesis, recently put forward again, that Caere hydriae are the work of Ionic artists (rather than of one single artist), immigrants into Etruria, is not at all improbable; production, however, can be localized, in that no amphorae of this kind nor vases of the same painters have been found outside Caere. A particular characteristic is the use of graffiti in the details, which is not so delicate as in original Ionic pottery."(1)

1. *G. A. Mansuelli,* Art of Etruria and Early Rome*, trans. C.E. Ellis (New York: Crown Publishers, 1965), p. 74. The most recent research seems to confirm the Greek character of these hydriae and tends to show that Greek vases were imported to Caere in large numbers from the first quarter of the 7th century to the middle of the 5th century. Willy Zschietzschmann (*Etrusques, Rome, *Payot) who studied this problem for many years, asserts that the potters of Caere merely copied imported Greek models, and even gives the names of some of these potters: "Potter of the Swallows," "Potter of the Bearded Female Sphinx," "Potter of the Rosaceous" or "Potter of the Braided Tails."*

The Tomb of the Reliefs—a replica of an Etruscan house

But the tomb that has yielded the most information on Etruscan household articles, and therefore on daily life in Etruria in the seventh century B.C., is the *Grotta Bella,* also called the Tomb of the Reliefs. Nowhere is the desperate need to perpetuate the appearances of this earthly life in the hereafter depicted better than here.

Guarded by two lions carved in the rock, a stairway leads to an underground room.[1] Numerous bas-reliefs decorate the walls. In the breadth of the walls, niches where funeral couches were stored are apparent. In the center of the rear wall is an immense niche containing two beds, those of the head of the family and his wife. Lightweight sandals, most likely belonging to that lady, are laid on a small bench. Beside it are a small table, a writing desk, and the knotted staff of the head of the household. Two sculptured colums bearing the likenesses of the man and the woman, depicted here with their weapons and jewels (bucklers, helmets, daggers, fan, earrings, and pendants), frame the two beds.

The two pilasters that support the ceiling of the chamber are decorated by a frieze in the round depicting a confused scattering of articles and animals, including instruments for hunting and fishing (slings and rods), kitchen utensils and tools, a card table, and

1. *This description is based upon the very handsome photographs of the Tomb of the Reliefs which illustrate Zschietzschmann's work,* Etrusques, Rome.

even a square container, probably for making cheese. As for the animals, two geese, one pig, a dog, and even a cat are easily identified. By its realism and details, the Tomb of the Reliefs allows us to enter into intimate contact with an Etruscan household.

"Ready for the eternal banquet of another world"

The Caere necropolis contains many other valuable remains. The rock-face *tomba della Cornice,* hewn out of solid rock, contains two magnificent carved seats, which appear to be two thrones intended for important members of some illustrious family. In this tomb, also known as the Casetta Tomb (Italian for "small house"), there are tiny rooms arranged in a row, separated by arched doors and windows, and the walls are completely bare. The sobriety and severity of this funerary construction gives this Casetta Tomb a surprisingly modern architectural look, similar to buildings based on the esthetic principles of Le Corbusier or Niemeyer, for example.

The two most beautiful and famous terracotta sarcophagi of archaic Etruria were also discovered in Caere. One now stands in the Villa Giulia Museum at Rome and the other in the Louvre. Both sarcophagi depict a couple stretched out on cushions. The man and the woman, according to the Etruscan custom, are together for the meal. The German archeologist Sibylle von Cles-Reden perceives the ancient Etruscans' image of the family in the harmonious and dignified bearing of these two couples—a family governed by order, tenderness, and fidelity, a far cry from the portrait drawn by the lascivious compiler Theopompus.

"To the patriarchal habits of the rustic Romans," writes von Cles-Reden, "whose womenfolk played a much less public part in life, this practice seemed altogether improper as did the prominent position of women in general among the Tyrrhenians .... But the numerous representations of such loving couples, united even in death, point clearly to the high regard in which marriage was held by the Etruscans .... Ready for the eternal banquet of another world (not yet, we must suppose, conceived in any dualistic sense at this period of the Etruscan nation's greatness), the couple sit on the couch in their finest array" (p. 39).

What if the key to the Etruscan language were to be found in Caere?

Despite the discovery of these marvels, the Caere (Cerveteri) necropolis has yet to yield all its secrets. A group of young archeologists from several European nations is presently conducting research under the auspices of the Cerveteri Government Archeological Excavation Office. According to a report published by this agency, researchers are currently attempting to rescue household articles, which constitute an extremely valuable source, as we have already mentioned, of a better understanding of ancient Etruria's "works and days."

"Today the Cerveteri necropolis," this report reads, "constitutes one of the groups of monuments most evocative not only of Italy but of the entire Mediterranean world. Besides the Tomb of the Reliefs, the Regolini-Galassi Tomb and the rock-face or Casetta Tomb, there are also numerous other groups of tombs that require long, painstaking research. The agency is increasing its efforts to improve working conditions for researchers and archeologists devoted to the Etruscan legacy. Indeed, excavations today require considerable financial and technical resources."

The report then notes the latest discoveries made at Cerveteri:

"One of the most recent tombs is in the shape of a hypogeum deeply hewn below ground level: its walls and pillars are ornamented with bas-reliefs of painted stucco depicting hanging articles and providing an evocative tableau of the weapons and instruments used in Etruscan domestic life .... The material coming from the tombs of this necropolis .... covers the period from the Iron Age to Roman times, with no solution of continuity .... It is quite possible that one day these excavations will provide us with a decisive artifact— for example a bilingual Etruscan-Latin inscription— which will, at last, impart to us the secret of the Etruscan language."

Tarquinia, the capital of Etruscan painting

Twelve and a half miles north of Caere (present-day Cerveteri) flourished Tarquinia, one of the oldest and most important Etruscan metropolises. Founded, according to legend, in the tenth century B.C. by the young Lydian hero Tyrrhenus, it was also the site chosen by the supreme god Tages, the founder of Etruscan religion, to reveal to his people the rites and precepts of his religion.(1)

Today Tarquinia (called Corneto until 1922) is a quiet, unassuming locality of 10,000 inhabitants perched on a small hill in the midst of olive trees. The modern town was built on the very site of Tarquinia's ancient necropolis where, since the nineteenth century, archeologists have been bringing to light innumerable painted tombs. The Tomb of the Augurs (530 B.C.), the Tomb of Hunting and Fishing (520 B.C.), the Tomb of the Lionesses (520 B.C.), the Tomb of the Triclinium (470 B.C.) and the *tomba dell'Orco* or Tomb of Hades (280 B.C.), just to mention the largest, offer the visitor a vast panorama of frescoes, the wide variety and unusual quality of which make Tarquinia the capital of Etruscan painting. Through these scenes of daily life recorded on the walls of funeral chambers, the mural paintings of Tarquinia allow us to penetrate 25 centuries of neglect and share the humble and secret concerns of a vanished people.

Etruscan love of life

What image of Etruria do these painting convey? In the tombs of Tarquinia, beside the scenes of banquets, feasts, and hunting depicting characters joyously pursuing the simple pleasures of life in the midst of a

1. *See the famous text by Herodotus that tells the story of Tyrrhenus, quoted in the first chapter of this work.*

luxuriant vegetation, there are somber portraits of the Kingdom of the Dead, ruled over by the baneful demons, Charun and Tuchulcha. As shown by the tomb paintings, the Etruscan individual held two absolutely contradictory beliefs: an anguished obsession with death and, simultaneously, an exuberant love of life. This split character makes him a mysterious and attractive individual.

The Tomb of the Triclinium magnificently renders the love of life so often shown by the Etruscans. The paintings were damaged by moisture and had to be removed under the care of the *Istituto centrale del restauro* to the Vitelleschi Palace (now the Museum of Tarquinia), where they can be viewed at leisure.

Upon entering the room in which they are pre-served, one is immediately impressed. The central panel is filled, even overloaded, with banquet scenes showing numerous couples reclining among pets and domestic animals. On the side panels are dancers; the men are dark and the women have pinkish-white skin. Their arms raised high in the air, they are whirling to a wild rhythm. The women's transparent tunics spin round their bodies, and the musicians themselves are giddy with the sound of their flutes and lyres. A reed-flute player dances with lyrical grace, his strong and supple body undulating.

The decor consists of shrubs and green or blue-green foliage against which these handsome bodies stand out, their silhouettes emphasized by the black line of the drawing or the border of their garments in a progressive color scale: white, pink white, pink, rose red, brown, black brown, black.

The Dionysiac feast of the Tomb of the Lionesses

The two themes, dance and music, may also be found in another tomb of Tarquinia, the Tomb of the Lionesses. Here the colors are more contrasted and the drawing is more subtle and lively. Many art historians consider this tomb's ornamental frieze to be one of the highpoints of Tuscan painting.

The feast, the frieze's central theme, is under the aegis of Dionysius, as the panthers, wine, ivy, and the dance itself that decorate the hypogeum are that god's symbols. This magnificent frieze overhangs the niche where the cinerary urn of the deceased was probably placed. Dynamic dancers are being driven by the beat of the music. A pleasant-looking, belly-shaped *krater* occupies the center of the panel. The *krater* is an egg-shaped receptacle for mixing wine and water, and it is therefore quite certain that the feast was in honor of *Dionysios-Bakchos.* Indeed, according to legend, the god of wine had tamed lions, panthers, and leopards.

Another ornamental motif emphasizes the Bacchic aspect of the banquet: a black pitcher with an elegant spout, placed at the extreme right of the painting. On each side of the *krater* is a musician: to the right, a flutist dressed in blue; to the left, a citharist dressed in white. The female dancer on the left is seen in profile and is dressed in a magnificent parade mantle with a light blue border. She is wearing an Ionian-style *tutulus.*

But the most picturesque scene is the irresistibly animated one depicted in the right portion of the frieze. Two dancers—a man and a woman—are performing together. The man has a reddish body and curly blond hair falling in long twisted locks. He holds a vessel in his left hand. The female dancer has a pinkish skin and brown hair, and is playing castanets. Two of her fingers are stretched out while the others are turned toward her palm. The movement of her arms and legs and the graceful pose of her feet are painted with great realism, proving that the artist had unusual gifts of observation.

Hunting and fishing scenes in Etruria

The Tomb of Hunting and Fishing also in Tarquinia, was discovered by Italian archeologists at the beginning of the twentieth century. It presents two other aspects of daily life in Etruria. Generally dated at the beginning of the sixth century B.C. (520-510), the tomb consists of two chambers.

Though the walls of the first chamber are unfortunately heavily damaged, one can still make out musicians and dancers moving among trees. In the second funeral chamber, the walls are painted with fishing and hunting scenes. Above the entryway are two horsemen returning from a hunt. Close by them, servants are busy. One is holding back some dogs scenting the undergrowth and others are carrying game hanging from a pole.

The sides of this second chamber are of stunning beauty. Air and water coalesce in a dream world. At the bottom of one of the panels, the blue sea is rippled by a gentle breeze. Fish and dolphins freely gambol. There are some young men fishing from a boat. In the air there are myriads of brightly-colored birds beating their wings. To the right of the landscape, near the boat, is a stratified boulder which hangs over the sea. From this promontory a young man with outstretched arms is aiming at a bird with his slingshot. In the small boat, whose hull is a dull red, there are two gaily animated young boys. One of them is leaning over the bow and carefully dropping a line of red string into the water. In front of him a dolphin, its body arched, is leaping in the sea.

Elsewhere a small boy wearing a blue shirt is trying to climb up a stratified rock, one side of which rises vertically above the sea, by grasping the sharp outcroppings. From this steep rock a nacked boy has just dived.

The painter caught the very moment when the diver's outstretched body is about to break the water. The boy's head is slightly thrown back. His joined hands and his locked legs and arms give an athletic rigidity to his body. The Etruscan decorator of the Tomb of Hunting and Fishing, without stepping out of the bounds of realism—a realism he was capable of reproducing because he enjoyed community life—draws us into his poetic world. Air and water become, by the persuasion of his talent, elements of the divine cosmos. Thus he fills this earthly paradise with a bright and playful fauna. Blue, red, and white birds outlined in black and green dash through the luminous air with outstretched wings. Wriggling fish can be seen under the pale, blue-green, swelling waves, rendered with violet traces.

In our opinion, this work is unique. It displays unusual realistic and poetic qualities peculiar to the

Etruscans of that period, men who were madly in love
with life.

Valuable source material about
the Etruscan pentathlon

The necropolis at Tarquinia, which proves to be a
sort of painted repertory of Etruscan daily life, holds
two other tombs whose friezes evoke a theme that was
dear to the Tuscans and highly prized during Greco-
Latin antiquity: the wrestling match.

In the Tomb of the Augurs, the two wrestlers have
black hair. The wrestler on the right has a V-shaped
beard, black like his hair. The one on the left, probably
younger, is heavier and clean-shaven. There is only
a black sideburn, half beard and half hair, crossing
his cheek vertically. The athletes' bodies are reddish
brown and clearly outlined by a brown line emphasizing their silhouettes. As in Homer's description, the two
antagonists are gripping each other face to face. The
younger of the two fighters, on the left, has seized his
opponent's wrists. The fight will be harsh, maybe even
fatal.

In the *tomba delle Bighe* (Tomb of the Two-horsed
Chariots), several scenes depict athletes in various
poses. They constitute valuable source material for
studying the games that were organized for the burial
of highborn personages—wrestling, boxing, jumping
and, in short, all the physical exercises included in the
pentathlon. For prominent Etruscan families funerals
were occasions for public displays full of pomp. Similar

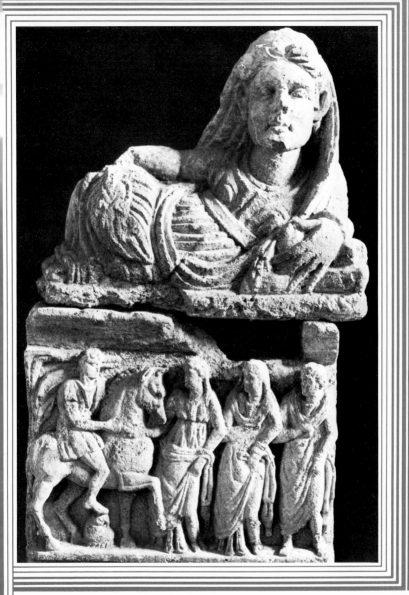

Etruscan funerary urn. On the base is a scene probably depicting an incident in the life of the deceased. The lid consists of a sculptural portrait of the deceased. *(Roger-Viollet)*

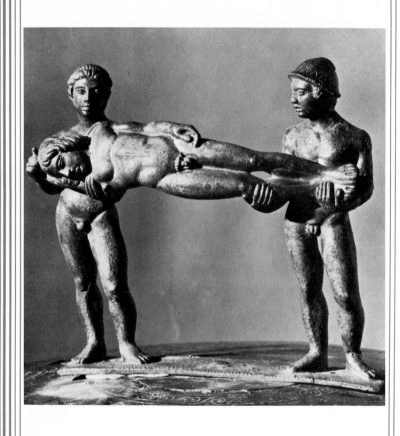

Lid of a bronze *cista* (chest) showing two warriors carrying a dead com
Fourth to third centuries B.C. Villa Giulia Museum, Rome. *(Rapho - Leonard vor*

customs were found in Greece and Asia Minor, and the luxury displayed for the burial of a prominent individual was no doubt a way to exhibit his power, his wealth, and the extent of his patronage. On the lateral surfaces of this tomb there are various scenes depicting athletes, wrestlers, and discus-throwers in competition.

The netherworld

The somber, pessimistic and nihilistic aspect of Etruscan civilization is illustrated in the Tomb of Hades. Dated 280 B.C. (that is, from Etruria's decadent period), the Tomb of Hades portrays the Kingdom of the Dead in a series of terrifying frescoes. The Etruscan individual who had, until then, managed to control his anguished fear of death throughout the vicissitudes of his tragic history, finally surrendered body and soul to it as it became evident that the Etruscan people were nearing their end. The ten centuries of its existence predicted by its gods and diviners would soon draw to a close.

The gods of the underworld are enthroned at the very opening of the tomb. Hades wears a wolf's skin on his head and is holding a snake in his hand. Next to him is seated Persephone, her hair writhing with snakes . . . . On the opposite panel, Geryon, a three-headed demon, is gazing upon Tiresias, who is meditating while surrounded by a multitude of short black figures—the spirits of the dead. Finally, we see Tuchulcha, the most threatening figure, an Etruscan demon with the face of a bird of prey and snakes tangled in his hair.

This is the procession of demons who are to inflict

the torments of the Etruscan afterlife upon the dead. The deceased's family had commissioned the artist to render this frightful vision with unmitigated realism. Thus, having reached the term of their destiny and conscious of its ineluctable course, the Etruscans allowed themselves to be engulfed by terror.

Trojans sacrificed by Achilles

Representations of this terror may also be found in Vulci, north of Tarquinia, in the famous François Tomb discovered in 1857 by the archeologists A. François and Noël des Vergers.

The most famous fresco—in any case, the one most often reproduced in art textbooks and catalogues— depicts one of the most tragic episodes of the Trojan War: the Trojan prisoners sacrificed by Achilles. This painting of the sacrifice of the Trojans is painted almost entirely in three colors: reddish brown, blue, and white. In departing from these colors and thanks to skillful gradations, the painter came upon paler composite tones of red and pink, as well as bluish tints derived from basic blue but sometimes almost white.

On the left side of the fresco we see the goddess Vanth, her two wings outstretched. Farther to the left, Patroclus—his head and body protected by one of the infernal goddess's wings—attends the sacrifice. He is dressed in a blue mantle which partially covers a striped red tunic. He has the painfully careless look befitting heroes who are being honored but who need no longer take part in mortal struggles. By sheltering

Patroclus' body under the wing of Vanth, the painter meant to personify the soldier's spirit.

Achilles, bending slightly beneath Vanth's other wing, is cutting the throat of an exhausted and nearly bloodless Trojan crouched at his feet. The face of the goddess is expressionless, devoid of the slightest passion. When the time comes, the merciless goddess impassively cuts the thread of life of those who have been sent to her. The face and gestures of Achilles are energetic. With his left arm he is holding his unfortunate victim by the hair; his right arm thrusts a sword into the poor devil's neck.

The demon Charun, who occupies the approximate center of the fresco, is grimacing and ugly. He holds a double-headed mallet. His hooked nose hangs over a wide mouth which is recessed so as to exaggerate his protruding chin. The infernal divinity's neck is powerful and thick—in short, monstrous. The pupil of his somewhat vaguely glaucous eye is situated near the nose, giving him a cruel, criminal expression. But to emphasize the horror inspired in mortals by this Charun, come purposely from Hell to preside over the sacrifice, the artist painted the face, neck, and arms of this loathsome divinity in a nauseating greenish blue. The cheeks and nose of this sinister figure are stained with cadaverous discolorations. Warriors on the right are dragging nude prisoners. No other fresco with such an intense feeling for death may be found anywhere.

The bestiary of an Etruscan Hell

Achilles, Patroclus, the Trojans—these allusions to Homeric legend serve as backdrops. Vanth and Charun preside in the foreground of this setting, for the drama they are performing relates not to a traditional afterlife born of Greek beliefs about death, but instead to a terrible and secret Etruscan afterlife. The admirable artist who depicted these Greek heroes has reshaped and recast them, so to speak, for his own artistic purposes. Moreover, he took great care to have Etruscan gods presiding over the ceremonies; here, they are commanders and judges of all. Fate, death, and the hereafter are no doubt themes common to many other peoples, but the artist was in no danger of contradicting himself by including the unfortunate victims struck down in countries other than his own; on the contrary, a common lot unites men everywhere as they face their inexorable destiny. The Etruscan artist dwelt upon the universality of death and hence he resorted to Homeric tales to support his own vision.

Above the great frieze, and in the lintels above the doors that open onto the other chambers, are decorations involving real and fabulous animals: horses, dogs, bulls, panthers, lions, felines, griffons .... A foal with a bristly mane is being harassed by two ferocious animals at its hindquarters and withers. In a bluish-gray area, a sphinx or winged griffon threatens an invisible animal with its hooked talons. These leaping beasts are drawn with precision and delicacy. The artist commissioned to portray the kingdom of the shadows had chosen his models from just about everywhere. The violent death and tragic destiny of heroes, and the presence of cruel, leaping creatures are standard themes in the Etruscan imagery of hell.

Scarce source materials of Etruscan architecture

Other tombs, scattered in other necropolises, contain innumerable painted frescoes which reproduce the works and days of ancient Etruria with striking realism. Though we know a great deal about Etruscan painting, the same cannot be said for its architecture. There are only a few physical remnants of the Etruscans' architectural genius: a few bridge foundations and several fortified enclosures. As will be seen, there are many sizable remains of funerary architecture. Yet the little that we do know of this architecture from the writings of Roman authors, in particular Vitruvius, the most qualified in this field, cannot but command our esteem.

The terms *templum tuscanicum, ratio tuscanica* and *cavoedium tuscanicum,* frequently found in Latin texts, evoke the conception of an original architecture, which had its own orientation system, and its own models, principles, forms, proportions, construction and dressing methods, and style of ornamentation. The Cloaca Maxima, the Capitol, and the walls built by Servius Tullius, whose solidity and layout still provoked the admiration of Imperial Rome, have been attributed to this architectural system; the honor of having created what was thereafter called the Tuscan order has also been ascribed to this system. Finally, Etruscan architecture is credited with the crucially important invention of the vault.

What can explain the near total disappearance of Etruscan monuments? This disappearance seems attributable to many causes: first, as Etruscan buildings used a great deal of wood, they were more vulnerable than others to weather damage or fire; in addition, war completely ravaged Etruria. We have noted too how harshly the Romans dealt with Veii, Vulci, and Tarquinia, burning and razing everything, devastating the sites of these conquered cities, and deporting their remaining inhabitants to guard against all future threats. During the desperate combats that marked the wane of Etruscan independence in the 3rd century, and later during the civil wars, more than one monument must have fallen by accident or in the violence of wholesale destruction.

It is therefore impossible to restore Etruscan architecture. Nevertheless, we shall try to determine the main characteristics of this architecture to see whether it deserves its reputation.

Volcanic stone, limestone and wood: the Etruscan construction materials

Besides wood, which will be discussed later, Etruscan architects used mostly volcanic stone and common limestone.

The former is abundant in southern Tuscany, Latium, and Campania. We know that at some time geological upheavals shook the entire region; between

Naples and Cumae there are more than sixty extinct craters. The Latium massif and, farther along the right bank of the Tiber, the massif between the river and the Radicofani Mountains near Chiusi, have lava deposits everywhere, as well as basaltic outcrops, hot springs, ash and scoria heaps, and craters transformed into lakes. All over this region the earth has been profoundly disturbed by underground fires. From these volcanic regions, Etruscans derived various construction stones including travertine, a yellowish stone of rather tough grain and slightly spongy in appearance; *peperino,* a grayish stone of petrified ash, which served to build Rome's oldest walls; and *nenfro,* a powdery-textured gray stone that takes on a whitish tint when cut.

As for limestone, it is found principally in southern Tuscany. There is a wide variety of limestones. Some limestones are dense like the *macigno* from Fiesole and Cortona; others are crumbly like the *cispo* from Chiusi which, however, hardens when exposed. Many are formed of conglomerate shells. These limestones, which are to be found almost everywhere at ground level and which formed the elevated masses on which the ancient cities were built, are the rocks that Etruscans most willingly worked with.

The Etruscans also used a great deal of wood. This is easily explained since the greater part of Etruria is covered with forests. There were woods on the slopes of the Apennines, at Chiusi, Perugia, and Arezzo; there were woods to the north near Pisa, south near Caere and Vosinii (Bolsena), without counting the famous Cimine forest which, as shown earlier, was used in a Roman strategy to penetrate to the heart of Etruria, whose people believed it to be an impassable barrier. Etruria was rightly reputed for its pines; it was a kind of Norway from which the sturdiest building wood was gathered. (1)

Did the Etruscans really invent the vault?

The scope of this book does not allow us to linger on the techniques used by the Etruscan architects. Nevertheless, it would be interesting to examine an often controversial point among Etruscologists: did the Tuscans invent the vault, as the Roman writer-architect Vitruvius implies? Basing his view on the study of certain Etruscan vestiges, particularly those of Veii and Populonia, Pallottino believes they did. Others, such as Bianchi Bandinelli deny it. The debate remains open.

Nevertheless, the most recent researches—especially those of the Viennese Etruscologist H.F. Pfiffig who has recently published (September 1975) a work devoted to Etruria—have established that though the Etruscans did not invent the vault, as it existed already among the Egyptians, the Chaldeans, and the Greeks, they used it with great effectiveness. There are two kinds of vaults, corbel arches and voussoirs.

A corbel arch is a course of stonework that has the appearance rather than the structure of a true vault. It is constructed of progressively overlapping horizontal blocks gradually narrowing to form an arch. As the

1. *Thus, when Scipio wished to improvise a fleet against Carthage, all the necessary wood was provided solely by the cities of Clusium and Volsinii.*

blocks are laid, the opening of the arch becomes so narrow that one stone suffices to close it. Once the course is laid in, the projecting corners of each squared stone are chipped off and thus a bay evoking a semi-circular or ribbed vault is attained.

Examples of corbel arches are not hard to find in Etruria. They may be found in Cerveteri, Tarquinia, Orvieto, and Cortona. The most remarkable one for its dimensions is that of the *Quinto Fiorentino.* Many are ribbed; some are rectilinear, notably those at Orvieto where the projecting stones have been carved so as to form a sharp angle; and others present alternating vertical and slanted sections.

As for vaults with voussoirs, they are, properly speaking, true vaults and consist of cut blocks of stone with wedge-shaped oblique joints disposed side by side so that they naturally rest upon each other and remain suspended in midair by the pull of gravity which, by exerting pressure on each stone simul-taneously, prevents their collapse.

The oldest remaining vaults are the ones from Veii (door of the Campana Tomb) and the one from Cortona (the so-called Cave of Pythagoras). The one from Veii was created directly from a corbelled course. All the joints are horizontal, except the ones closing the bay at the top; rather than laid on flat like a kind of lid, this one was cut in the shape of a keystone and was inserted in the empty spot left by the last two stones of the corbel arch. Actually it is not a keystone, since it does not support anything and it alone is supported. It completes the structure but it is not an essential element; its role is merely to fill up an opening.

As for the Cortona vault, it consists of five monolithic blocks over 10 feet long, cut in oblique joints, sort of enormous voussoirs that span the entire length of the burial chamber. But these monoliths are merely false voussoirs. Rather than supporting each other their extremities are resting on a semicircular block that fulfills the function of arch and carries the weight of the structure.

Despite the Etruscans' taste for this type of course, it did not play an important part in what may be called its architecture of monuments. It did not fit within the architectural scheme of their public or private, religious or civic buildings; neither their temples nor their houses included vaults. For them the arch was only a convenient device, a successful engineering expedient, applied only to roadwork, city gates, sewers, funeral chambers, and the retaining walls of underground galleries. Moreover, before the Romans no one had fully grasped the wide use that could be made of the vault and the bold architectural combinations which it made possible.

The main types of Etruscan woodwork

Though the Etruscans were experienced in carving and fitting stone, they used, as we have observed, a great deal of wood in their constructions. Most of their private and public buildings were dressed in woodwork, of which nothing now remains. Fortunately, however, while cutting their tombs into solid rock and carving their sarcophagi and funerary urns, the Etruscans reproduced the appearance of their houses or their temples and thus conserved the aspect of their roofs and ceilings. With this source material, the archeologists have been able to describe the main types of woodwork.

The simplest type of woodwork consisted of intersecting horizontal members, arranged in two rows of parallel crossbeams laid perpendicular to each other. At the intersecting point, the members were slightly notched so as to interlock. This arrangement is easily observed in certain tombs of Vulci.

The coffer was also related to this system. Two parallel beams were placed perpendicular to two other parallel beams. A third set of beams was laid parallel to the first but slightly recessed. Beams are alternately superimposed two by two in one direction or the other, gradually narrowing the distance between each pair of parallel beams until the opening which remains is small enough to be filled up by a batten or a tile. As with the preceding woodwork, all the members are fitted *à mi-bois.* Flat bands or *doucines* (cymas or ogives) are then nailed to the ends of the beams and along the reentrant angles to stop up the gaps.

But there are other types of woodwork which consist not of intersecting horizontal members, but of slanted members. The main member is a beam spanning e entire length of the chamber. Rafters, joined by twos *à mi-bois* and whose extremities rest on the ridges of the lateral walls, are placed at intervals on this beam. The framework of a twin-sloped roof is thus created. This type is ordinarily called the echinus timber.

When the dimensions of the chamber are very big, instead of one sole beam, there are sometimes two arranged parallel to each other and supported by one or two pillars, as in the Tomb of the Tarquins at Cerveteri. These two main beams are connected by horizontal joists arranged as in a floor.

The most complicated systems are those utilizing a hip. Two horizontal frames of different sizes are connected by four projecting members going from the four angles of the larger frame to the four angles of the smaller frame, so that the smaller frame is at a certain height above the larger one. The skeleton thus created is reinforced by several adjoining intermediary members.

As for parasol supports, they are made of slanted members wedged at the top and converging toward a central main beam into which they interlock. The spacing of these members is maintained by horizontal struts distributed into several concentric rows. This system has the aspect of a lamp-shade or an umbrella.

A pediment: a sea-god between two winged genies

In fact, the Etruscan architectural element of which we have the most information and of which numerous remains have survived is the ornamentation.

As with the other peoples of Mediterranean and Oriental antiquity living under the sun's blinding light, which destroys perspective, the Etruscans understood the advantage of emphasizing the contours of their architecture with projections and shadows, to fix the viewer's gaze and give it landmarks, so to speak. Ornamentation offered a resting-point for the eye and responded to a taste for magnificence, decoration, and brilliant detail so often displayed even today among the peoples of southern climates—a kind of ornamentation synonymous with bad taste only to those who have never lived under the bright light of sunny countries. The Etruscans possessed this predilection for vivid ornamentation to the same degree as the Egyptians, Assyrians, Phoenicians, and Greeks. Like them they delighted in enhancing their simple buildings with rich decorations.

Where there were stone surfaces, the Etruscans readily chiseled in ornaments, not merely moldings but also bas-relief figures and objects. Thus a tomb at Sovana has a sculpted pediment decorated with a sea-god and two winged genies. In Norchia there are pediments, modeled after Greek temples, that bear figures in their tympana and on the walls of the entryway behind the columns. Also to be found in the Tomb of the reliefs at Cerveteri are relief sculptures, carved as if hanging on the walls, of the various objects that constituted the equipment and utensils of a wealthy Etruscan household. A great many similar works bear witness to the Tuscan architects' taste fot this mode of decoration.

The infinite resources
of the Etruscan art of monuments

Buildings were also decorated in color, which once again indicates the ancient Tuscans, pronounced taste for painting. Polychromy was very important in the sepulchral chambers. The walls were framed by painted borders, as were the outlines of the doors, and the framed areas were covered by various compositions using bright, even vivid, colors. In some of the tombs of Caere, all of the utensils in relief were enhanced by the use of colors reproducing their actual appearance. The doors were surrounded by moldings with alternating red and black slanted bands. Almost without exception, the funerary urns were painted; the survival of coloration on some of the architectonic details proves the existence of polychromy in monumental art. On one hut-urn in Tarquinia, the supports of the roof are set off in white, and white zigzags and sinuous lines are painted at intervals. The same white color has been used underneath the cornice to draw out a frieze of zigzags underlined by a horizontal stripe; still further, white is used in squares and notched stripes to heighten the uniformity of the woodwork for the doors and windows.

The visible portion of Etruscan woodwork is covered by a color-wash designed not only to hide the bareness and irregularities of the wood, but also to protect its surface against weather damage. In underground tombs, where the ceiling is hewn from solid rock, beams or coffers are reproduced in the rock; these structurally useless pieces are made of wood and are overlaid with paint, probably to imitate true supports, and the tones are varied in such a way that the different elements of the roof and ceiling may be distinguished from one another, a decorative effect made possible by the variety of and contrast between light and shade.

Among the Etruscans there was another decorative system, this one using applied ornamentation. Instead of carving the surfaces of walls or decorating them with coats of plaster, ornaments were brought in and nailed to them. The most common ornamentation was of terracotta, clay being the substance most readily worked by the Etruscans and the one they used with the greatest skill. In Orvieto, Civita Castellana (Falerii), and Luni, there are statues and bas-reliefs in the pediments, plaques attached to the walls (either in the middle of the wall, like the painted plaques at Caere, or on the friezes); Gorgon masks, flower-shaped ornaments, or Sirens attached to the ends of the coffers; Gorgon masks, ram's heads, or rosettes, all nailed into the corners of the tympana; and finally antefixes placed on the edges of the roofs, at the extremities of the rafters.

Sometimes the applied ornamentation was made of metal instead of terracotta. Vitruvius writes of pediments decorated with statues of gilded bronze. In accordance with a custom observed in Asia Minor and Greece, round shields of bronze or gilded bronze were hung in the tympana of the pediments or along the walls. This explains why imitation shields were found in several Etruscan tombs in Norchia and Perugia. The bronze shields found in the Regolini-Galassi Tomb, fashioned from a single sheet of metal and much too thin to have been of use as defensive weapons, had a purely decorative function. This must also have been the purpose of the convex discs, found in Tarquinia, that bear the mask of a bearded and horned Bacchus at their center.

Following a practice common among oriental peoples, the Etruscans also used metal sheets for stone-dressing. At Chiusi there is a sepulchral chamber where the ceiling is made of bronze panels; another chamber at Chiusi appears to have been decorated with gold leaf appliqués. In Veii, the walls of a burial vault are virtually tapestried with bronze to the height of about 10 inches. The examples of the Regolini-Galassi couch and of an Etruscan chariot found in Perugia, with its wooden frame wrapped in a sheet of hammered bronze, indicate that the Etruscans were given to making metallic sheaths. In any case, we do know that they customarily plated the entire surface (or at least the borders) of their doors with sheets of bronze. This is clearly visible on a large number of funerary urns and painted murals where even nailheads were taken into account. Large bronze rings, sometimes suspended from the snout of a lion, were used as door knockers or handles.

There was thus a wide variety of decorative styles. Reliefs, colors, ceramic and metallic appliqués—all the resources or ornamental art were used to break the monotony of the structures and to enhance the bare buildings with bright detail.

The tomb with a burial chamber and the advances of Etruscan funerary architecture

In addition to this tremendously rich and inventive ornamental art, we have a reasonably good knowledge of Etruscan funerary architecture. The "most religious people of antiquity," as the Etruscans were described by writers of antiquity such as Livy and Cicero, have left us thousands of examples of this funerary architecture. Without reviewing the religious notions that explain the profusion and wealth of these funerary monuments, we shall now describe several aspects of this funerary architecture and define the different types of burial places.

In southern Tuscany, particularly in the vicinity of Civita Castellana (Falerii), Veii, and Sutri, there are hillsides with high sheer cliffs whose surfaces have been smoothed by man, made perpendicular and marked at intervals by holes which, from a distance, appear to be loopholes in a fortification or pigeonholes. But they are actually burial places. Some of them are quite small, intended only for cinerary urns. Sometimes the urns are arranged in no particular order; at others they are lined up or stacked like files. They are usually sealed with tiles. (1)

At Veii, one can also see niches hollowed out in the same way in the middle of a cliff, but they are much

1. *These niches are believed to be the oldest form of what the Romans later called* columbaria. *At Toscanella, there is even a perfectly formed* columbarium. *Unfortunately, it is not certain that it dates back to the Etruscan period, and as it has been emptied of all its funerary furnishings, it is impossible to date and identify its origin.*

larger than those discussed above and have enough room to hold a corpse stretched out to its full length. Some of them are rectangular and wider than they are high; others are semicircular, still others are cone-shaped. All of them are empty today and there are no artifacts to help us determine the historical period they represent. They were formerly closed by slabs which completely sealed off the opening; there is sometimes debris remaining from these slabs.

But Etruscan funerary architecture did not really reach its peak until the tomb itself took on the charac-teristics of a room or burial chamber, with a more or less stylized arrangement that indicates architectural intent. This type of burial place is found only excep-tionally in circumpadane Italy, perhaps also because the Etruscans of the Po Valley had no direct contact with the oriental peoples whose use of vaults as burial places was part of a secular tradition and who quite probably passed the idea along to the southern Etruscans. (1) The fact is that at the very time when oriental influences became dominant in central Italy, entombment in burial chambers became popular in Tuscany. It has been found throughout that region and remained in use until the end of Etruscan civilization.

There are burial chambers dating from throughout the period between the sixth and second centuries B.C. Some were constructed of masonry of either polygonal rubble or squared stones, and their vaults were built with corbel arches or voussoirs. But most of them were

1. *Current excavation projects seeking to determine the different styles of Etruscan funerary architecture seem to indicate that those supporting the oriental theory of the Etruscans' origin are correct.*

hewn directly into the sides of hills close to cities or atop which the cities were built. Access to them is gained by a long sloping corridor, a stairway, or a more or less deep shaft, with holes driven into the walls at intervals for descent by hand and foot.

Burial chambers dating back to the seventh century B.C.

The most basic type of burial chamber is the passageway-type tomb peculiar to the necropolis at Tarquinia. This type consists of a trench modified into a burial chamber, with a small walkway used for entry. Some of the chambers measure nearly as large as the trenches themselves. Thus while the trenches were 6.5 feet long and 4 feet wide on the average, several of the chambers measured 6.5 feet on one side. In general, they are a little larger and average 10 by 8 feet. Running the length of their walls is a bench to support the unburned cadaver with its funerary furnishings. It often happens that one of these burial chambers will contain several bodies. The room is bare and contains no ornamentation.

This very simple and very ancient variety (several of these tombs in Tarquinia date back to the seventh century B.C.) has always been in use in Etruria. Its use persisted in Tarquinia until the Roman era, but it was changed slightly. In particular, the size was increased so that what was once a passageway became a chamber nearly 16 feet long and over 9 feet wide. When this occurred, such a chamber had a bench not only along each lateral wall but also along the wall opposite the entryway.

Burial chambers of this type are found not only in Tarquinia, but almost everywhere in Etruria, in Chiusi and Vulci, for example. In Chiusi and Orvieto, the walls of the burial chamber are often made of masonry with a barrel-vault, probably because the tufa seemed too porous and soft to hold without some support. Sometimes, as in Orvieto, the sides of the chamber were strengthened by a double thickness of walls, the space in between filled with a mixture of clay and gravel, probably to prevent seepage. Some burial chambers at Chiusi and Orvieto are arranged in a special way: across from the entryway a pilaster projecting from the wall forms a partition and divides part of the chamber into two compartments. Generally speaking, the simple burial chambers are rectangular or square, although they are not always precisely proportional.

Some of these funeral chambers may be of an imposing size. One chamber found in Chiusi, for example, measures 72 feet on one side. The Regolini-Galassi Tomb in Cerveteri, noted for the paintings and artistic treasures mentioned earlier, has a passageway nearly 6.5 feet wide and about 65.6 feet long, which is devided into two chambers. In Tarquinia, the so-called Tomb of the Cardinal is a square room measuring 60 feet on one side, supported by four large pillars about 6.5 feet high. Its ceiling is quite low, so low that a moderately tall man can just barely stand erect inside. This disproportion between the height and the breadth gives the impression that it is even larger than it is. The

Tomb of the Typhon at Tarquinia is 43 feet long, 33 feet wide, and 13 feet high. A square pillar measuring 6 feet on one side stands in the center. One of the rooms of the Tomb of the Tarquins in Caere is 36 feet square. The Tomb of the Triclinium and the Tomb of the Reliefs are rectangles measuring 26 by 23 feet. At Volterra the chambers are ordinarily circular and have a large square pillar in the center. Their diameter ranges from 33 to 82 feet.

In addition to these tombs with a large single burial chamber, many burial places in Etruria consist of several chambers, which are interconnected and constitute something resembling an apartment, a more or less faithful reflection of the dwellings of the living. This practice was in conformity with the Etruscan belief in a "second life" after death.

Labyrinths to baffle thieves

Because of their variety, it is impossible to survey all the types of sepultures with multiple chambers. Most of them consist of two or three chambers, as the Casuccini Tomb in Chiusi, for example. The Tomb of Isis at Vulci has four rooms, whereas the cave of the Sun and Moon and the François Tomb have eight. The Volumnii family sepulture at Perugia contains ten. Sometimes several burial places dug out of the same hillside are connected by narrow, winding corridors, alleys so to speak of these underground cities. These corridors, dug out in all directions and often with sudden changes of ground level, seem to have been constructed not only to afford access to deeper points within the tufa, but also to impede the searches of grave robbers by means of their meandering, which was often as complex as a labyrinth. Passageways of this kind are found in the Poggio Gaiella necropolis near Chiusi, and their discovery was widely discussed because the labyrinth was thought to be part of the famous Tomb of Porsenna, king of Clusium.

In the multichambered burial places, the relative position of the chambers is not always the same. Sometimes they are hollowed out at different levels, with the first chamber serving as a vestibule to the funeral chambers proper, which are reached by a cave shaft, stairway or well. In others, eyerything is on the same level. Sometimes the rooms are partitioned and open along both sides of a corridor like the cells of a monastery. At other times they are in sequence, that is, the first is used for access to the second, which in turn must be traversed to reach the third. The most common variety have chambers arranged around a large central room, much like the layout of Roman dwellings with their *Cubicula* around the *atrium*.

This wide variety of combinations was a product either of the type of terrain, the need to respect the funeral galleries previously dug in the vicinity, or of a multitude of special rules difficult to determine.

The opulent Tomb of the Reliefs at Cerveteri

Now that the shapes, dimensions, and arrangement of Etruscan funeral chambers have been indicated, let us turn to a closer examination of the interior decoration of some of the chambers, which are interesting from the standpoint of architectural detail. Consider, for example, the Tomb of the Tarquins in Cerveteri.

It is a far cry from the burial chamber with four bare walls, benches along the sides and a flat or barrelled ceiling. Here the bench is double, that is, it consists of two broad steps. All around the chamber the walls are pierced at regular intervals by rectangular cavities wider than they are high, which form a continuous series of thirty-five niches, some of which can hold two bodies each, side by side. These niches are separated from each other by pilasters bearing detail work painted red. Beneath each alcove, colored lines were used to draw a wooden bed with a low stool at its foot; apparently there was an effort to reproduce the appearance of a bed in an alcove. (1)

Two massive square pillars, themselves decorated by colored drawings, rise up in the middle of the room. The portions of the ceiling they each support are cut into the tufa so as to simulate two major beams extending the full length of the chamber. Simulated rafters are there as well, highlighted by red lines and covering the space between the beams and the walls parallel to them, reproducing the interior appearance of a twin-sloped wooden roof. In the ceiling between the two pillars is a shaft providing a direct connection between the chamber and the surface. Notches are arranged at intervals to provide handles and footholds for those climbing down.

1. *The stucco on which most of the details were painted has fallen away in many places, and only a faint trace of the decoration remains.*

The arrangement of the Tomb of the Reliefs at Cerveteri recalls that of the Tomb of the Tarquins, with only a few modifications of detail and a more sumptuous ornamentation. Like the Tomb of the Tarquins, this one has one bench, two square pillars, and niches carved into the walls. But the bench is on one level rather than having two steps and, in addition, is far broader than the ordinary benches in Etruscan burial chambers, which are often nothing more than a narrow ledge parallel to the wall to hold bodies (or small sarcophagi as at Volterra). Here, however, the bodies must have been laid out at right angles to the walls. Low ridges on the surface of the tufa mark off the space to be occupied by each body, and indicate that along this bench there were thirty-two contiguous funeral couches.

There are thirteen niches or alcoves, each representing a bed with its pillow carved into the tufa and painted dark red. They are separated from each other by a fluted pilaster with a scrolled capital with lotus flowers. Above the niches and along the edge of the ceiling runs a frieze decorated with sculpted and painted weapons of all kinds: helmets, swords, shields, and greaves. Above the entryway the frieze is decorated by an offering dish for libations and two bull's heads adorned with ribbons, remembrances of the sacrifice accompanying the funeral.

Along the doorposts and on the pillars, also in relief and color-enhanced, a multitude of domestic objects are reproduced: armor, harnesses, toilet articles, crockery, and household pets including a dog, a goose, and a turtle.

The niche opposite the entryway, at the other end of the room, is adorned by a splendidly decorated bed. When the tomb was discovered it still contained the skeleton of a warrior in his armor. This was the place of honor, the location occupied in the house by the marriage bed, and hence called the *lectus adversus*. As the tomb was an underground image of the Etruscan house, this location was probably reserved for the head of the family. The bedposts are finely carved and brightly painted. At the foot there is a low stool, behind which may be seen figures of Cerberus and Charon portrayed on the wall. Immediately to the side, the tufa is cut to represent the front of a sort of chest covered with metal brackets and closed with a lock.

Porsenna's Tomb: an unsolved riddle

In the field of Etruscan funerary architecture, one of the questions which continue to intrigue specialists is the riddle of the Tomb of Porsenna, the celebrated king of Clusium referred to earlier in this book. In antiquity this tomb had already acquired the reputation of being one of the wonders of Italy. Here is Pliny's description of it, found in his *Natural History*. The information provided by Pliny is based on a work by Varro, the famous Roman grammarian:

"I shall in describing the building make use of the very words of Marcus Varro himself: 'He is buried close to the city of Clusium, in a place where he has left a square monument built of squared blocks of stone, each side being 300 feet long and 50 feet high. Inside this square pedestal there is a tangled labyrinth, which no one must enter without a ball of thread if he is to find his way out. On this square pedestal stand five pyramids, four at the corners and one at the center, each of them being 75 feet broad at the base and 150 feet high. They taper in such a manner that on top of the whole group there rests a single bronze disk together with a conical cupola, from which hang bells fastened with chains: when these are set in motion by the wind, their sound carries to a great distance, as was formerly the case at Dodona. On this disk stand four more pyramids, each 100 feet high, and above these, on a single platform, five more.' The height of these last pyramids was a detail that Varro was ashamed to add to his account; but the Etruscan stories relate that it was equal to that of the whole work up to their level." (1)

To be sure, this description has set modern imaginations spinning. Utter phantasmagoria! says one. Poetic fantasy, says another, extracted from some old Italian epic and become a formal tradition. Colossal electric machine! says a third. Still others, less skeptical, acknowledge the partial truth of the description and suggest that more or less accurate restoration efforts be made. Translating the terms of this description into a structure, however, one might picture something resembling a huge dais, a sort of dome-shaped construction with projecting canopies like the brim of a hat, supported by five slender, pyramid-shaped pillars. The four pillars at the corners would be higher than the dome of the dais, standing erect like needles or

1. *Pliny*, Natural History, *trans. D.E. Eichholz (1938; rpt. Cambridge: Harvard University Press, 1962), Bk. XXXVI, 19 (pp. 91-93).*

masterheads. The dais or cupola would have been made of wood and covered by metallic ornaments, following a technique widely known by Etruscan architects. As for the upper platform with its five 250-foot pyramids, it seems completely implausible.

In fact, despite the strange appearance of Porsenna's monument as a whole, it does in some respects parallel some funerary structures in Etruria. A structure with a square base supporting five conical towers, four at the corners and one in the center, may be seen to this day along the Appian Way near Albano. It is the monument known (somewhat arbitrarily) as the Tomb of the Horatii and the Curiatii. Its origin is the subject of much controversy. Some think it is the tomb of Porsenna's son Arruns, who was killed in 504 B.C.; others say it is the tomb of the great Pompey. The workmanship of the masonry tends to indicate a period somewhat nearer to the final years of the republic. In any case, its appearance is so unlike traditional Roman architecture that this monument may be considered to be a reproduction of an earlier type, probably Etruscan. The analogy with the tomb of Porsenna is striking. (1)

Was there a particular orientation for Etruscan sepulchers and necropolises?

Another puzzle is the object of concern on the part of Etruscologists—the orientation of the sepulchers.

1. *A team of American archeologists is currently engaged in excavation at Chiusi. Will the riddle of Porsenna's tomb soon be solved?*

Would a people that was, as we have seen, so devoted to religious practice, magic, and prodigies, have overlooked this question? Did they fail to do for the dead what they always did for the living when, as we have noted in numerous examples, they took care to make the dwellings of the dead as similar as possible to those of the living?

It seems there is no risk of error in asserting that Etruscan necropolises were therefore not laid out in total disregard of any rules of orientation. But here lies the root of the problem. What were these rules? Were they applicable to the necropolis as a whole, somewhat like a city to be founded, or to each sepulture individually or, even further, to each of the bodies laid out in succession within the same tomb? Were these rules of orientation based on reference to one of the four cardinal points of the compass, or instead on some geographical relation to the city of which the necropolis was the silent mournful colony?

It is impossible to resolve all these questions. In examining the layout of Etruscan cities and their surroundings, it is impossible to determine what feature to concentrate on. There are no consistent relationships with a given point on the horizon; necropolises and sepultures are pointed in all directions—north, south, east, west, and all points in between. There is no consistent relationship with the position of a city: at Caere (Cerveteri) the tombs are north of the city, and at Tarquinia they are to the south. Elsewhere they are to the east or west.

If one city is examined separately, it can be noted that no specific area is set aside solely for sepultures. They are found almost everywhere in the vicinity. At Bieda, for example, they border almost all the valleys that converge at the city. If all the tombs in the same locality are surveyed, the necessary conclusion is that each one is oriented in a different way. At Civita Castellana, for example, where the tombs are hollowed in the tufa of the hill upon which the ancient city of Falerii once rested, their openings face in all directions depending on the topography. This is also true of the town of Poggio Gaiella, near Chiusi. At Vulci, where the tombs open onto a long corridor, some of them have entryways opposite those of other tombs, meaning of course that they are oriented in opposite directions.

The bodies do not seem to have been oriented in any particular direction either. In one and the same chamber, some are laid out parallel to the entryway and others at a right angle to it. At Volterra, the urns are arranged in a circle around the room. At Castel d'Asso, there are groups of trenches at the center, and trenches fanning out in all directions. We are forced to conclude that only the nature and topography of the land led the Etruscans to select one location rater than another and use one orientation rather than another. It all boils down to a simple matter of topographical convenience.

Does this mean that any orientation theory must be rejected? No, but one may be retained only on condition that the word "orientation" be limited to mean only a group of ceremonies intended to set the boundaries of the selected site and to claim it in a religious manner. This is the procedure by which

Romulus, after selecting the hill where he wished to found Rome, outlined its boundaries in accordance with the rites of the Etruscan *templum*. Orientation then becomes a sort of consecration of the choice, which itself was made with the greatest of freedom and for the sake of convenience. As current controversies among Etruscologists indicate, however, the question is far from resolved.

"Between these points, temples and wild lands be mine for direction, for viewing, and for interpreting"

While the orientation of sepultures and necropolises is still a matter of debate, this is not the case for the temples. All specialists agree on this issue, saying that Etruscan religious architecture is governed by strict principles regarding orientation.

Furthermore, a text by Festus provides us with some of the Etruscan restrictions concerning the foundation and consecration of altars and sanctuaries. These prescriptions are so precise that they set the minimum number of sanctuaries that each city was to have; just as in the outside wall there had to be at least three doors, within the city there had to be at least three temples, one dedicated to Jupiter, one to Juno, and one to Minerva. (1)

Like the number of sanctuaries, the space set aside for them is determined with precision. The space

1. *This question was examined during the earlier discussion of Romulus' foundation of Rome.*

selected is generally on a hilltop from which the entire horizon can be seen and which, in turn, can itself be seen from all sides. It was easy to detect a similar situation in Etruscan cities, which were always built on hilltops or plateaus. Once the choice was made, the religious official in charge of the orientation ceremonies, i.e., the soothsayer, followed a ritualistic procedure and circumscribed the area being consecrated.

Varro has recorded the contents of one of these formulas:

"Temples and wild lands be mine in this manner, up to where I have named them with my tongue in proper fashion.

"Of whatever kind that truthful tree is, which I consider that I have mentioned, temple and wild land be mine to that point on the left.

"Of whatever kind that truthful tree is, which I consider that I have mentioned, temple and wild land be mine to that point on the right.

"Between these points, temples and wild lands be mine for direction, for viewing, and for interpreting, and just as I have felt assured that I have mentioned them in proper fashion." (1)

Inside the area he had thus set aside by his sacramental speech, the soothsayer waited for divining signs such as lightning or the overflight of birds, which would be tantamount to indications of the gods' willingness either to approve or disapprove the choice of location which the soothsayer had temporarily

1. *Varro,* On the Latin Language, *trans. Roland G. Kent (1938; rpt. London: William Heinemann Ltd., 1958), Bk. VII, 8 (p. 275).*

claimed. If the choice was not approved, another location was sought and the same procedure was started anew. If it was approved, everyone remained: the location then became sacred and assumed the name of *fanum* (sanctuary). From that moment forward, it became the property of the god to which it had been consecrated and could not be changed without that divinity's formal consent.

Vitruvius and the construction of an Etruscan temple

In accordance with religious requirements, Etruscan temples were built on a high place so that, as noted above, they dominated the horizon. Like most Greek temples, their foundations were on a natural or artificial platform which raised them even further. Several of these platforms may still be observed in locations in central Italy. Some were cut directly into the rock, and others were constructed from fitted blocks.

Dionysius of Halicarnassus described the enormous foundations on which the temple of the Capitol was built, foundations which were admired by the Romans and which Pliny thought extravagant. To make them it was necessary to scrape the rock, construct terracing, and build retaining walls, traces of which still exist. The temple was thus built on what resembles an immense pedestal with steps; that is the way it appears in bas-reliefs and on coins. The walls were substantial, probably constructed of squared and fitted stones, as was so often the case in the necropolis of Orvieto, or using the procedure common to the Etruscans, whereby stones were placed sometimes lengthwise and sometimes at right angles to the others. The walls were ordinarily quite thick: at the Capitol the foundations discovered indicate a thickness of approximately 13 feet for the partitions separating the *cellae*; the same type of walls were 6.5 feet thick at Civita Castellana, whereas the outside wall measured almost 10 feet.

The walls of the *cellae* were windowed. In fact, among the objects found in the ruins of Civita Castellana were plaques of terracotta set in frames and carved so as to admit light, with extremely elegant plant ornamentation giving them the appearance of embellished grillwork. As for the columns, Vitruvius describes their appearance and proportions as follows:

"At the bottom these columns are to have a diameter one-seventh of the height. (The height is to be one-third of the width of the temple.) The top of the column is to be diminished one-fourth of the diameter at the bottom. The bases are to be made half a diameter high. Let the bases have their plinths circular and half the height of their base, with a *torus* [round molding] and *apophysis* [or congé, the curving away of the shaft against the base] as deep as the plinth. The height of the capital is to be half a diameter. The width of the abacus is as great as the diameter of the column at the base. The height of the capital is to be divided into three parts, of which one is to be given to the plinth or abacus, one to the echinus or ovolo, the third to the hypotrachelium [necking] with the congé."

We lack the space here to go into details on the construction of an Etruscan temple. Noted specialists have devoted extraordinary studies to this subject. (1) We will confine ourselves to a further reference to Vitruvius, the architect who left us a good description of the construction of a Tuscan temple. Here is his description :

"Above the columns, beams are to be placed bolted together, of such proportionate depth as shall be demanded by the magnitude of the work. And these coupled beams are to have a thickness equal to the necking at the top of the column, and they are to be so coupled with dowels and mortises that the coupling allows an interval of two inches between the joists. For when they touch one another and do not admit a breathing space and passage of air, they are heated and quickly decay. Above the beams and walls the mutules are to project one-fourth of the height of the column. On the front of these, casings *(antepagmenta)* are to be fixed and above them the tympanun of the gable either of stone or wood. Above this ridgepiece, rafters and purlins are to be so placed that the pitch of the roof is one in three." (2)

1. *See, in particular, the works of Raymond Bloch, Albert Grenier, Bianchi Bandinelli and above all, Jacques Heurgon, the eminent Etruscologist who was kind enough to grant me an interview and to spend many hours explaining the mysteries of Etruscan architecture to me. I wish to thank him here.*
2. *Vitruvius,* On Architecture, *trans. Frank Granger (1931; rpt. Cambridge : Harvard University Press, 1962), Bk. IV, ch. vii, 2-5 (pp. 239-241).*

A white bull and white cow, harnessed to a bronze-bladed plow

The architectural skills of the Etruscans are apparent not only in the construction of temples but also in the structure of their cities and the ramparts surrounding them. Altough, as we have noted in this regard, archeologists have had to settle for scant and rare evidence, there has been a partial but successful reconstruction of the principal elements of the civil, and especially the military, architecture of the Etruscans.

The fortresses built by the Etruscans in Tuscany and Latium during the period of their greatest power are totally unlike primitive entrenchments. No more embankments, ditches, or stockades; instead there are solid walls built of squared stones, rising up on hilltops and constituting, to some degree, an extension of the slope. Instead of cities with low buildings, there are acropolises.

After having chosen the site for the city to be constructed, the Etruscans performed a special cere- mony for temples, which has been described in numerous Latin texts. Before building the walls, it was necessary to trace the line along which they would be raised. The founder of the city, in sacred vestments and with his head veiled and toga lifted up, attached a white bull and a white cow to a plow, the bull on the right and the cow on the left. The plowshare was made of bronze. The plowing was done according to certain rituals and in a given direction, so that the bull always walked outside the line of the future wall and the cow on the inside. As the plow advanced, great care was taken to throw the clods of earth turned up to the inside of the furrow. At intervals, where the gates of the city were to open, the furrow was interrupted by lifting the plow.

The area thus marked off was sacred, and no one had the right to enter it. Roman tradition reports that Remus brashly committed such a sacrilege and paid for it with his life. The ancient texts leave some room for doubt as regards the pattern the plowshare was supposed to etch into the earth. If Plutarch is deemed reliable, it was a circular shape, but the term *Roma quadrata*, which designated Romulus' old city on the Palatine, implies a rectangular shape.

The Etruscans as masters of military architecture

Whatever their shape, all the cities of which remnants may be found in Etruria today appear to have been powerful citadels; the Etruscans were thus masters of military architecture. Their defensive structures were so remarkable that they excited the imagination of the ancients, and the Etruscans were attributed the honor of having invented the art of fortification. Dionysius of Halicarnassus, who reports this tradition to us, adds that according to some authors the names of "Tyrrheni" and "Tyrseni" were applied to the Etruscans because of their skill in constructing towers.(1) This etymology does not seem very sound, but at least it bears witness to the powerful impression left by

1. *In Greek, the word for "tower" is* turseis.

Etruscan cities, perched like aeries atop steep slopes which made them hard to approach.

Furthermore, as we have observed, the Romans several times had occasion to test the solidity of these fortifications. The siege of Veii, it has been noted, cost them quite an effort. They had to besiege it for several years; Roman tradition, doubtless exaggerated by legend, mentions ten years, the same period as for Troy. Ending the resistance which the blockade had not weakened was too great a task for all the energy of Camillus; it was necessary to resort to a surprise attack, amassing all the besieging forces in the center of the square and seizing the ramparts from within.

All of Rome's wars against Etruria resulted in long, arduous sieges. Fidena was besieged eight times; Volsinii did not surrender until a famine afflicted the city; Volterra long resisted Sulla, and Nequinum, according to Livy's account, was taken only when it was betrayed by one of its residents after a long blockade.

When crossing central Italy and observing the sites where Etruscan cities once stood, the traveller is forced to admire the skill with which the sites were chosen for defensive purposes. It is hard to imagine positions more powerful than those of Cortona, Volterra, Orvieto, and Fiesole. Volterra and Cortona are 1,800 and 1,650 feet above sea level, respectively; Orvieto is 1,050 feet above sea level, Fiesole 980 feet, Arezzo 950 feet, and Perugia 1,650 feet.

The fortified perimeters of the Etruscan cities were not highly developed. The largest of them all, at Volterra, was, according to its remaining portions, only

24,600 feet in circumference. Apparently this was the approximate perimeter of Veii if, as Dionysius of Halicarnassus maintains, that city covered an area comparable to that of Athens. According to the computations of Georges Dumézil, Athens had an approximate circumference of 4.4 miles, excluding Piraeus and the ports.

Most of the other Etruscan cities, traces of which may be found in various places, typically covered an area with a circumference ranging from 1.2 to 2.5 miles (Populonia, Saturnia, or Cortona). They were quite small cities and could scarcely have held more than a few thousand inhabitants. It is a great surprise to find that these cities, which played such an important part in the Roman wars and resisted the Roman legions for so long, covered such small areas of ground!

Fortresses suspended over chasms

What were the principles behind building these ramparts? It is nearly impossible to completely reconstruct all the details. Their ruins are so rare or in such bad condition, or even so constricted between modern structures, that there are no precise data and the researcher is most often forced to base his reasoning on conjecture.

Nevertheless, two systems of fortification may be distinguished, one without, and the other with, towers. The first type is represented by the walls of Volterra, Populonia, Cortona, and Saturnia. Cursory examination of the massive and odd-shaped bulk of these walls clearly reveals that, of the two systems, it is the first one which dates back the farthest.

The walls rise up on the more or less steep slope dominated by the city. Their height varies: sometimes the walls drop and sometimes they rise as they follow the undulations of the rocky outcrop. It is important that the walls be based on solid rock so as to prevent besieging forces from undermining them. The enclosure has a smooth surface without any kind of protuberance. There are no outside ditches. Instead there are broad, deep ravines, sometimes natural and resembling chasms (like those at Volterra) and sometimes straightened and cut by hand-held picks, as at Civita Castellana.

Approach is difficult from any direction. It is necessary to scale steep slopes that, even today, may be climbed only with difficulty by following endless sharp bends, often passing between enormous upright boulders. The wall itself is truly unassailable, exactly the factor that made the presence of towers unnecessary. Lacking a point of support on a flat surface, the enemy was unable to breach the wall. The fortress thus suspended over a chasm was so well defended that it could be overcome only by a blockade or a surprise attack.

It is difficult to say exactly how high the walls were. Sections still standing at the Volterra and Saturnia sites are from 33 to 36 feet high, but it is obvious that several of the upper layers are missing. The top of the wall was probably crenelated. The bas-reliefs on two urns found in Volterra, which picture the siege of Thebes, show a wall which in fact was crenelated and had a fortified gate. It happens that one of these gates corresponds exactly to the ruins of a gate at Volterra. It is hence reasonable to conclude that we are looking at one corner of the Volterra enclosure and that the walls were crenelated at the top.

The walls were not of uniform thickness. At Rusellae, the wall appears to have been nearly 10 feet thick. At Volterra, where the wall consisted of two parallel layers with the space between packed with gravel and other material, it was nearly 17 feet thick. At the Palatine it measures about 8 feet. A 6.5-foot thickness is generally accepted to be the minimum.

Cosa, the city with sixteen towers

The second system of fortification consisted of curtains of rampart flanked by bastions. It is this system that may be seen at the ruins of Cosa. This city near the coast is on an isolated plateau at an altitude of nearly 1,000 feet. The enclosed area follows the ridge of the plateau, which it borders on all sides. The present height of the walls ranges from 10 to 33 feet and they are about 10 feet thick. A breastwork sheltered the defenders from the blows of attackers.

There are fourteen towers, irregularly placed along the surfaces of the fortress. The north and east faces have only one tower each; there are five towers on the south face and the other seven are all on the west face, which looks toward the sea and which was probably considered to be the most vulnerable. The towers are square and of different sizes: their average width was 26 feet and they projected an average of 10 feet out from the rampart surface. They were deep enough to protrude into the interior as well. Two other towers must be added to the other fourteen; they are flush with the outside wall and have only a rounded protrusion toward the interior square.

There are three gates, one on the north face, one to the south, and the third to the east. The west face, the most vulnerable one and the one with the most towers, has no outside opening.

The substantial water works of the Etruscans

Etruscan genius must be credited with the immense hydrological projects carried out in a country that is one of the worst havens of malaria in the world. If the Etruscans were able to prosper there it is because, by dint of their patience and tireless efforts, they succeeded not in eradicating but at least in correcting the unhealthy conditions in the country. Since the entire problem stemmed from excess water, which neither ran off toward the sea nor was absorbed by the ground and hence lay stagnant in low-lying areas, the Etruscans had to concern themselves with drying out the plains. The numerous excavation projects in Etruria and the Roman countryside show the care with which outlet and drainage canals were maintained in antiquity. As early as the nineteenth century, when work on railroads in the Maremma Mountains and the Roman countryside required cutting large paths which exposed the substratum, a large number of underground conduits traversing the fields were observed.

Proof of the ingenious and venturesome activity of the Etruscan people in this regard is found in ancient traditions. Pliny, describing the estuary of the Po between Ravenna and Altinum,(1) points out the immense bypassing, diking, and channeling projects executed by the Etruscans in the vicinity. The port of Atria (now Adria) was probably built by them. Several passages by Strabo also seem to indicate that the Arno was controlled at its mouth by the Etruscans since early antiquity.

The Etruscans were concerned not merely with ensuring the healthfulness and systematic drainage of the plains on which they farmed; they also cared about the hygiene of their cities and developed a sewer system to evacuate all unnecessary water from the city. Many of these sewers still exist. Some are hollowed out of solid rock, as in Sutri, Civita Castellana, Orvieto, and Saturnia. Others are partially constructed from masonry, like those in Volterra and Fiesole. Most of the sewers are very narrow, but some are wide enough for a man to pass through. This has given rise to the idea that they might have been used for several purposes, either to take water out of the city or to make raids, to provide defense or supplies in time of war, or to allow secret communication from one place to another within the city.

---

1. *Ancient city located in the most remote part of the Venetian lagoons, whose population took refuge at the site of Venice during the barbarian invasions.*

The Cloaca Maxima, masterpiece of Etruscan architecture

Among the sewer systems attributed to the Etruscans, there are two which are still nearly intact and which bear witness to their highly advanced art. One is located near the mouth of the Marta at the site of Gravisca, the former port of Tarquinia, and the other is the Cloaca Maxima of Rome.

The Gravisca sewer was discovered in the nineteenth century by the famous British consul, Dennis, who recognized it beneath accumulated silt and dense vegetation, which hid the approaches to it. It is one of the finest specimens of vault work conserved in Etruria. The voussoirs are nearly two meters thick; the arch is of the springing stone variety, and the masonry work was done with great care, having even joints and no cement.

As for the Cloaca Maxima, it differs a bit in construction from the Gravisca sewer. Instead of a single arch supported by springing stones, the vault is characterized by three rows of superimposed voussoirs, constructed with perfect smoothness and using no cement or spikes. The ancients greatly admired its masterly sense of order and unshakable solidity. "The magnitude of these projects," notes Livy, "could hardly be equalled by a work even of modern times." Pliny, for his part, writes: "They are pounded by falling buildings, which collapse of their own accord or are brought crashing to the ground by fire. The ground is shaken by earth tremors; but in spite of all for 700 years the channels have remained well-nigh impregnable."(1) What most struck ancient writers was the size of the structure. Pliny points out that the arch was large enough for a chariot loaded with hay to pass beneath it.

The Cloaca Maxima, after so many centuries, is still used today as a sewer for an entire section of Rome. Recent investigations have shown that it crossed the width of the Forum at the level of the Julia Basilica. It remains to be seen whether it is really as old as Roman traditions would have it. They claim it was built during the reign of Tarquin the Elder. But it has been observed that in many places the vault is made of travertine blocks, a construction material never used in the structures of the royal period. The workmanship indicates a relatively recent period.

Whatever its age, the Cloaca Maxima is one of the masterpieces of Etruscan architecture.

The Greeks bestow the envied title of "Friends of the Arts" on the Etruscans

With the exception of a few rare examples such as the miraculously preserved Cloaca Maxima, there are only a few remnants of Etruscan architecture. On the other hand, Etruscan sculpture has left a substantially larger number of traces, which establish again that this secretive and superstitious people cultivated the art of sculpture with extreme refinement.

Early in their history the Etruscans enjoyed shaping

1. *Pliny,* Natural History, *trans. D. E. Eichholz, Bk. XXXVI, 24 (p. 106).*

materials. When they were still a semibarbarous people, they endeavored to make objects other than pots and basins. They had vases shaped like animals and tried, with mixed success, to model figurines from clay. Not content with clasps made of bent and twisted bronze wire, they came up with fibulae which had decorative curved sections representing a coiled serpent or even a horse and rider. All of this speaks more for their intentions than their experience, but it is the mark of a nascent plastic sense.

With time, this sense developed and strengthened. Hands became more skilled and worked on the widest variety and most difficult of materials. More models were available thanks to imports from Asiatic and Greek trade. There were workers free to copy, interpret, and modify them by amalgamating various styles. Soon these workers flooded Italy with products from their own shops: the plunder of Volsinii provided the Romans with as many as two thousand statues. The day came when the Greeks, so proud of their own art, stopped scorning the work of Tuscan craftsmen and bestowed on the Etruscans a title they would have preferred to keep for themselves, that of "Friends of the Arts" *(philotechnoi).*

Canopic vases, marks, antefixes, and storytelling tiles

Of all the common or precious substances bestowed on man by nature, clay seems to have been preferred by Etruscan sculptors; when modeling it they exercised their talents to the fullest. The ancients often praised the terracotta statues made in Etruria. When the kings of Rome erected a sanctuary to Jupiter on the Capitol, they sent for Etruscan artists to decorate it with clay statues. These statues have disappeared, but time has spared many others which enable us to see what ceramic sculpture in Etruria was like.

Almost every museum has some curious examples of Etruscan terracotta sculpture. The Louvre collection includes the group of sarcophagi from Cerveteri, a monument from the end of the sixth or the early fifth century B.C. which is more or less contemporaneous with the famous statues of the Capitol. The museum of Florence has the so-called *Larthia Seianti* sarcophagus, as well as several decorative statues found at the sites of temples that have disappeared from Luni, Orvieto, and Civita Castellana, and a countless number of sarcophagi of all ages and sizes, so-called canopic vases with a human head serving as a cover, masks, antefixes, and storytelling tiles, not to mention thousands of black vases in relief.

Clay may be worked in various ways. Sometimes it is set in molds, which are used to pull numerous copies of the same piece. This is the case for many flat figurines, antefixes, masks, cinerary urns, and sarcophagi, which are produced by groups of workers. Sometimes the form is made by hand and the model itself is fired; occasionally the fingerprints of the worker and the blows of the chisel are visible. This is how most of the portraits decorating the canopic vases and the prize sarcophagi were shaped. No mold could have yielded such fine features, such fluidity of draping, such a tangle of fringes and folds as those characterizing some statues.

The two procedures are often used concurrently, as all the rather large statues were not made as a single unit but of separate sections, worked with more or less attention to detail depending upon the importance of the piece. The arms, hands, and feet were generally sacrificed, with the artist devoting his efforts to shaping the head and the characteristic details of the costume. On the Caere sarcophagus, for example, while the faces are noteworthy for their precision and the individual details of physiognomy, the arms are scarcely shaped at all and more closely resemble pieces of wood than limbs. They are actually only appendages, which sculptors probably had an assortment of, molded in advance, in their workshops.

The variety of materials used by Tuscan sculptors

But the Etruscans sculpted stone nearly as often as clay. To achieve full awareness of the bold chiseling approach used by Etruscan sculptors working directly with solid rock, one need only recall the façades of Castel d'Asso, Bieda, Sovana, and Norchia, and especially the magnificent bas-reliefs in the chambers of the Tomb of the Reliefs at Caere. There must have been many stone statues, considering the number of animal figures (such as lions and sphinxes) that have survived in a relatively well preserved condition; the statues of seated female figures, an archaic type calling to mind the mother-goddesses of Greece; and the covers of sarcophagi and urns.

Countless bas-reliefs are also available. In addition to those on sarcophagi and urns, which number in the hundreds, there are several *cipi* [exterior funerary stone monuments] decorated with figures and found in Chiusi or thereabouts, and a number of historiated steles, most of which come from Bologna. For Etruscan sculptors, all types of stone were considered equally good. They used stones of smooth or rough texture, yellow or gray chalky tufa, hard marbles, soft alabasters, and dense or porous volcanic rocks.

Often the rock used was not solid enough to make the statue in one piece. This frequently occurred at Chiusi in particular, where the *cispo* is so crumbly that a fingernail can easily cut into it. Most of the statues made in or near Chiusi therefore involve fitted pieces (arms, feet, heads) which are interlocked by means of holes deliberately dug out for that purpose and whose joints the sculptor did not even take the trouble to mask. These appendages are somewhat haphazardly held on by means of fasteners.

Tuscan sculptors also used bronze, and there are thousands of statues extant, especially bronze figurines. The most remarkable of them are the Orator, in the Florence Museum, the *Mars* of Todi, *Minerva* and, of course, the marvelous Chimera of Arezzo, reproduced in thousands of art books.

We have no knowledge of what wood sculpture was like in Etruria. Pliny mentions an image of Jupiter made of wood from a grapevine in Populonia, and a statue of Vegoia made of a cypress tree on the Capitol at Rome.

On the other hand, a few ivory sculptures have been found in Etruria, such as a portion of elephant tusk carved in the shape of a pail, discovered in a tomb at Chiusi. Further examples include the four coffin plaques now in the Louvre, which depict a chariot drawn by two winged horses, a hunting scene, a banquet, and the sea god Oannes from Assyrian mythology.

Finally, amber was also one of the substances used by Tuscan sculptors, as verified by the magnificent heads found at Marzabotto, near Bologna in Great Northern Etruria, among other items.

The sarcophagi—the luxury of ceremonial pomp

It would be inconceivable to study in detail the thousand marvels of Etruscan sculpture in this space. We must limit ourselves to pointing out a few of its exceptional successes. In the field of funerary sculpture, an area in which Etruscan production is both abundant and varied, the sarchophagi hold a privileged position. Among the Etruscans, the sarcophagus was not just a common casket or anonymous coffin. It has a name, shown in its inscription, and a face, that of the deceased. On top of the base enclosing the body itself, there is a lid bearing a statue.

The body was laid out in the sarcophagus as in a bed, and it was natural that the statue would recall such a position, given the mental association made between slumber and death. On a large travertine urn found at

Tarquinia, the deceased may be seen lying on his back, dressed in the full costume of a Bacchic priest and having that god's attributes, a *cantharus* and a *thyrsus* [cup and ivied staff]. Near him stands a doe. His eyes are not quite closed, but everything suggests that sleep is near.

A similar position is seen on several of the sarcophagi found at Caere and Tarquinia as well as on a multitude of small terracotta urns now in the museums of Chiusi and Florence, which seem to have been cast in a single mold and on which a child wrapped in a blanket is sleeping.

Finally, there are two remarkable sarcophagi from Vulci showing a married couple lying together face to face, amorously embracing in their marriage bed. One of these sarcophagi is executed with great flair and may be considered one of the most remarkable works of Etruscan statuary dating from the late fourth or early third century B.C.

Still other figures atop sarcophagi are lounging as if on a divan, with their legs idly stretched out and their upper torso raised up and leaning on the left elbow, which in turn is resting on one or two cushions. These figures have one or several objects in their hands, such as an offering dish, a drinking vessel of some kind, a fruit, an egg or one of the symbolic foods offered to the dead; or perhaps a mirror, a fan, a scroll, or some tablets. Sometimes the bed contained only one person; at others, when the sarcophagus was designed to hold two bodies, there was a couple. Most of the figures have a radiant mien. The couples seem to be abandoning themselves to the intoxication of the meal and sometimes are shown in postures bordering on the lascivious.

The figures are dressed for celebration; there are always multicolored clothes, garlands, crowns and jewels. The bed itself is by no means ordinary. Whenever the sarcophagus has been shaped or painted in such a way that details may be distinguished, the image is of a handsome piece of furniture with historiated wood carvings, cushions, and luxurious soft drapery— in short the luxury of ceremonial pomp.

Winged demons seizing an apparent prey

The bas-reliefs decorating the sides of the sarcophagi almost always have as their theme death and the voyage of the soul to the netherworld.

One sarcophagus now in the museum of Florence depicts an elderly man, who has just died, lying on a bed. His two children, one of whom seems to be guided by a benevolent genie, are approching him to perform their final duties. One of them, a young woman, is closing his eyes. A spirit of death, armed with a sword, is waiting in the corner of the scene.

On one sarcophagus from Vulci, two winged demons, their arms circled by serpents, are coming to seize a girl as if she were the prey of Death. Her father is interceding and holding her back, and her mother, accompanied by her smaller children, is vainly calling to the spirits of death for mercy. Elsewhere we witness the final farewell of a married couple taking leave of their parents. The woman who is to die and whose

statue is on the cover of the sarcophagus is being
dragged away by a winged demon grasping her by the
arm, while at the other side of the bas-relief another
genie holding a lit torch is leaving the funeral chamber
as if he had just finished preparing a space for the
deceased.

A funeral procession

On the principal surfaces of a cinerary urn shaped
like an *aedicula* [miniature temple], also found at Vulci,
is the representation of a funeral procession. One of the
bas-reliefs shows the deceased, wrapped in a shroud
and with his parents seated beside him on a four-
wheeled chariot, traveling to his final resting place. A
driver seated at the front of the chariot is handling two
mules, at whose heads walks a slave. A dog is walking
with the procession and the soul of the deceased is
floating above the mules in the form of a bird. The
procession is continued on the other bas-relief, which
depicts a retinue of hired female mourners preceded by
a flute player.

Then follows a procession of victims to be sacrificed
at the funeral rite. At the head of the group marches a
person who is either a sort of herald or the lictor, armed
with a staff. Behind him are three captives in chains
carrying the articles required for the ceremony. Then
come veiled women, followed by armed men leading
mules and a dog. Two rams and two oxen follow the
procession.

Charuns and Furies anxious to carry out their heartless task

On other sarcophagi, Death travels on horseback, or on the neck of a sea monster, or in a chariot pulled by a team of horses. In this sinister journey he is almost always accompanied by one or more Charuns and funeral genies, armed with swords or mallets, who in turn are pulling the team by the bridle or follow it closely as if they were afraid their prey might escape.

In the pictorial realm we have seen evidence of how the Etruscans' somber imagination delighted in representing the most sinister aspects of the carriers of death. Everywhere we see hideous, grimacing Charuns brandishing clubs or mallets, or winged Furies armed with torches or serpents. All these genies of the king of the underworld, anxious to carry out their heartless task, eager to cut short the effusions of tenderness and despair, crowd the bedsides of the dying, use threats to precipitate the moment of the final embrace, or speed the work of the shadowy figures they are escorting so as to hasten the moment of departure on the voyage of no return.

It seems that the sculptor is trying to render, in as gripping a manner as possible, the bitterness of death, the wrenching pain of separation, the sudden blow which fells men in the midst of their joys and the things they love, the mysterious force that tears them away from life and takes them to the shadows of a terrifying unknown.

"The ghastly mask of death"

The theme of death, which fascinated the Etruscans, is also found in the field of glyptics, another area in which Etruscan artists excelled. Certainly the engraved stones found in large numbers at Vulci, Tarquinia, Sutri, and Populónia often reproduce Greek mythological themes, such as a satyr pursuing a nymph, Neptune and his trident, Minerva fighting the giants, a winged Victory with a palm leaf. But the dominant, obsessive theme is death—death and the sojourn in hell. Here again we see Charun, Tuchulcha, and their loathsome servants swarming about. Here also they become excited, grimace, and subject the dead to a thousand torments.

André Piganiol has written quite correctly that "Etruscan art, at each stage of its evolution and in every one of its fields, wears the ghastly mask of death."

Printed in Switzerland
Published by Ferni
Distributed by Pleasant Valley Press